Learning Through Art

Learning Through Art

Recipes for Childrens' Art Activities

Faith Tadman

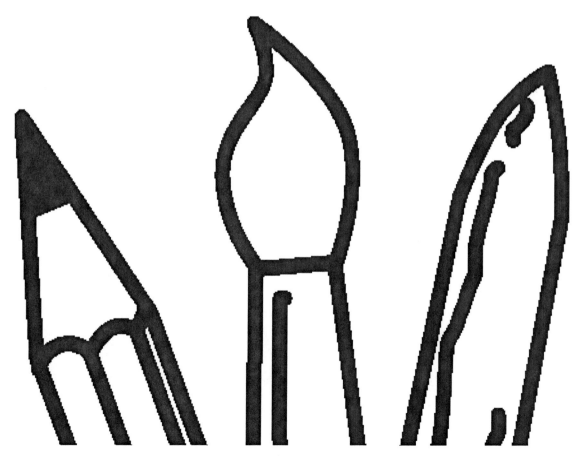

HUMANICS LEARNING
Atlanta -Frankfurt-Paris

HUMANICS™ LEARNING

Humanics Learning Publications are an imprint of and published by Humanics Publishing Group, a division of Humanics Limited. It's trademark, consisting of the words "Humanics Learning" and the silhouette of a young girl in a circle, is registered in the U.S. Patent Office and in other countries.

Humanics Limited
PO Box 7400
Atlanta, GA 30357-0400

Printed in the United States of America

Library of Congress Catalog Card Number: 99-067133

ISBN: 0-89334-300-5

Table of Contents

Preface..vi

Chapter One   An Introduction..1
Chapter Two   Fun With Crayons and Chalk........................ 6
Chapter Three   Let's Collage... 13
Chapter Four   Pleasure With Paints.....................................24
Chapter Five   A Multitude of Manipulative.......................... 41
Chapter Six   Junk Art...52
Chapter Seven   Art To Eat..68
Chapter Eight   Seasonal Art.. 80
Chapter Nine   Let's Dress Up... 97
Chapter Ten   A Plethora of Paper Plate Projects.............109
Chapter Eleven   Nature Art...122
                   Pattern Section..137
                   References

PREFACE

This project began when my two oldest children Louis and Heather were preschoolers and I began to save their art work and the craft and art ideas that accompanied them. Later after my daughter Rachael was born in 1990 and we moved to Seattle, WA I continued this project (at a very slow pace) and used the ideas in this book (with great success) in my Home School Preschool Program that I operated for over seven years. Many of these projects have also been tested on an after school child care program that I was in charge of as well as a Brownie Troop that I was in charge of for three years.

Some of these projects came to me from loved ones and friends such as Sharon Bryant, Toshie Honjo, Sylvia Anderson, Michele Leggett, Michelle Steinberg, Debra Tadman and Carol Valentine Gregor who shared their love of art and creativity with their children as well. Some of these projects have been handed down to us and the original creator of the ideas are unknown. Still other projects are born from my imagination and that of my creative children and their creative father Steven Tadman.

The art projects in LEARNING THROUGH ART are presented in a recipe style format. The supplies are listed first and the instructions follow. This enables the parent to easily determine if they have all of the supplies beforehand. This book is intended to be a recipe book of art projects.

Children love doing art and the art projects and processes in this book have helped to develop many of the positive attributes such as creativity, emotional expression, problem solving, hand-eye coordination and language acquisition to name but a few, in my three children.

Enjoy LEARNING THROUGH ART A Recipe of Children's Art Activities with your children but most of all remember to SPEND TIME with your children and ENJOY YOUR CHILDREN they grow up very fast!

CHAPTER 1
An Introduction to Art

Art for the young child embodies a great many applications. Art is more than crayons, scissors, and paste. This medium is a way for young children to express feelings that are otherwise too difficult to verbally express. It is also a way for the young child to have a sense of control over his/her environment and to learn to master skills. What a sense of achievement it is for a young child to learn to hold and cut with a pair of scissors! Much hand eye coordination and patience comes with learning this skill.

` Art is also a way of learning that is subtle yet so exciting. What amazement it is for the young child to learn that blue and yellow make green! There are as many ways of learning as there are different types of art mediums. How good it feels to work with clay, and better yet to pound it when we are feeling out of sorts with the world.

In addition to the expression of feelings through art, this medium also helps to build creative thinking in young minds. Since there usually are no hard fast rules involved in art experiences, children are encouraged to problem solve. There are several factors, however, that are important in fostering creativity for the young child.

* Always remember that the process is more important than the finished product. Many children are usually more interested in what they are doing while they are doing it than the outcome of that experience.

* It is also best not to interfere while the child is involved with the art experience (there is a big difference between offering helpful suggestions and being intrusive.)

* Allowing enough time for the art experience is essential. Nothing stifles creativity more than having to stop a project before the child has completed his or her exploration.

* Variety is in fact, THE SPICE OF LIFE! Not all activities are suited or appeal to all children, so therefore, it is important that they have exposure to a variety of art experiences.

* Lastly, keep in mind that these art experiences can influence your child's love and appreciation for creative experiences through out their lives.

Since children have such a sense of pride in their creations, their art work should be displayed for all to see. Refrigerators work nicely for this. (The child can help to create a magnetic refrigerator frame.) Homemade calendars with the child's favorite art is also a way to display art and a great gift giving idea during the holidays. It is also essential that the child's name be written on his work. All artists sign their creations.

Encouragement is also a primary ingredient for successful art experiences with the young child. As with all of us, a little bit of praise can go a long way. Praise can also help the young child to feel like his art work is special and, indeed, it is! Please refrain from asking "What is it?" This can really deflate a young artists pride. A more appropriate response would be to ask "What were you thinking about when you drew this picture?" or a statement "What beautiful colors you have used !" These positive statements do in no way undermine your child's self-esteem.

This book is an attempt to help give you the parent or early childhood educator an opportunity to do fun yet meaningful art experiences with your children. It will also provide many hours of fun and exciting kid proven art projects as well. All that is really necessary are a few basic materials and a little (or perhaps a lot) of patience with your child. Messes will happen as you proceed on but the clean up process is just as important a part of the art as the project itself.

Doing art with the young child in your home can be an easy and rewarding adventure for all concerned. Materials need not be elaborate. In fact, saving found materials in your home can help to reduce the minimal cost even further. The following is a list of found materials around our home than have been useful in creating many exciting projects:

paper plates	egg cartons
toilet paper rolls	roll on deodorant bottles
clean meat trays	yogurt containers
wrapping paper	lunch bags
aluminum foil	wax paper
frozen juice can lids	paper cups
straws	cotton balls
yarn	q-tips
packing peanuts	small boxes

In addition to found materials that are used around your home, food products can also be used for a multitude of creative activities. No need for bored children around the house. The following is a list of food products that have been very helpful for art projects in our home:

cornstarch   cornmeal
cream of tartar   flour
salt   rice
food coloring   whipping cream
pudding   shaving cream
pasta noodles   food coloring
cereal with o's   beans (not recommended for
                      children who put everything into
                      their mouths)

These found materials can be used to help supplement your already existing collection of art supplies. A youth size table and chairs is a worthwhile investment for art with the young child. They can be purchased at second hand stores for a reasonable amount. Your collection of supplies can be stored in a handy tote when they are not in use.

The following is a list of art supplies that we have found to be a real must:

glue

paste

tape

construction paper

paint brushes

crayons

scissors*

newsprint

masking tape

paint smock (old shirt-dad's will do)

markers (CRAYOLA now

tempera paint

has a brand of washable

(black, white, red, yellow, blue)

markers)

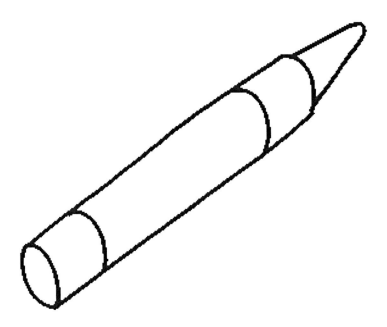

*Scissors for young hands can be purchased at department stores, toy stores, craft shops, or teacher supply stores. If your child is left-handed, scissors for lefties are sold at teacher supply stores. These stores also sell scissors for the beginner cutter. There are several varieties now on the market. Good scissors are essential. It is very frustrating for a child who is trying to master cutting skills to have an inferior pair of scissors. Use Fiskars for children beginner cutters and the pointed type of scissors for the more experienced cutter.

   Once you have collected all of your art supplies it is time to begin doing art projects with you child. What a splendid activity for a rainy day, or a helpful way to entertain your child when you have things that need to be accomplished (some of the activities require more supervision than others).
   The rest of this book will be presented in sections according to the type of activity involved as well as the types of materials used. It is my hope that this book will provide you and your child with many hours of pleasurable art experiences!

Ideas that worked for me.

Please send us ideas that work for you.

Humanics Learning PO Box 7400 Atlanta, GA 30357 • www.humanicslearning.com

CHAPTER 2
Fun with Crayons and Chalk

CRAYONS and coloring books are synonymous with childhood. Crayons for the young child can be in and of themselves a very creative tool. A little ingenuity can take the creativity one step further. It is my belief that traditional coloring books can stifle a child's creativity. Coloring books usually have all the work done for them. There is not much creativity involved in just coloring in spaces that someone else has already created. When children are given blank paper and crayons, they're encouraged to create their own designs The occasional use of coloring books will not be a negative influence on creativity. Children can be encouraged to add their own designs to coloring books. There are now coloring books available on the market that allow the child the opportunity to create their own pictures.

When purchasing crayons, be sure that they have been certified as nontoxic. Crayons that are safe meet performance established by ANZI Z356.1 and conforms to ASTM D4235 and will state this information on the container. Crayons without this information may be toxic to your child.

Look for the following seal when you are purchasing crayons for your child.

Broken up crayons without wrappers can be used in a multitude of ways. At our house crayons are always undressed. There is something in the feel of a crayon without its wrapper. Crayons without their wrappers can be used for crayon rubbings. Don't discard those broken crayons because they can be recycled. Use small paper cups, cupcake paper, or candy molds. Place several small pieces of broken crayon in the cups. Place these on a cookie sheet in a warm (250() oven until the wax has melted. Remember when removing these from the oven that the wax is HOT! Set in an undisturbed place to dry. Presto special crayon rubbing crayons.

CRAYON RUBBINGS

flat objects
paper
crayons with their papers

Crayon rubbings are created with a flat object laid underneath the paper and the side of the crayon is rubbed over the paper. As a child, we use to put quarters underneath paper and rubbed over the top with a pencil. This is the same principle. Many objects can be used to create exciting designs for the child. Greater success will be achieved if flatter objects are used. Leaves of different varieties, rocks, coins, shapes cut from cardboard, puzzle pieces, flat cookie cutters are but a few suggestion for items that may be used. Different textured materials will also make for some interesting crayon rubbings. The ability of rubbing with the side of the crayon is one that will require time, patience, and practice. Sometimes the objects that are being rubbed move around. Taping the object or the paper down can help alleviate this frustration. Use your creativity and imagination and have fun!

CRAYON STENCILING AND TRACING

sharp crayons   tape to hold down the stencils
paper   objects to trace
stencils

Stenciling is another enjoyable activity that can be done with crayons and paper and a few objects with interesting shapes. Cookie cutters or puzzle pieces work well too. Cardboard can also be cut into a variety of shapes to be used for both stenciling and tracing. The object behind stenciling is to have the child draw or color inside the cut out designs. Tracing, on the other hand, would have the child tracing the outside edges of the objects used from stenciling.

Some interesting shapes for the young child to trace are body parts. Body tracing is a fun activity to do at least every six months. The children are amazed at how much they have grown. The children have fun adding details to their bodies. Hand and foot tracing are also very satisfying activities for the young child. We like to trace our outstretched arms and hands and then connect the lines in the middle and write THIS IS A GREAT BIG HUG FROM HEATHER! We then cut out the hugs and send them to Grandparents who live far away who especially love getting these hugs!

CRAYON NOTCHING

drawing paper
wrapperless crayons
butterknife (used to notch the crayon)

Crayon notching is a fun and easy way to color. This type of coloring usually puts my children in the mind for Fourth of July fireworks. As added inspirations for my children's creativity, I sometimes provide patriotic music and pictures of fireworks. To create a crayon notching all that is needed is paper and crayons. The unwrapped crayons are then notched. This is an area where mom and dad need to assist. A butterknife usually makes a nice notch. Be sure to put several notches on each crayon. The notched side of the crayon is then rubbed over a piece of paper. The notched sides of the crayon leaves negative lines of spaces on the paper. Remind the child to keep the notched side to the paper.

CRAYON MURALS

crayons
large piece of butcher paper of shelf paper
tape (masking tape works well)
long wall and a group of children

Crayon murals are a fun activity to do with a group of children. To create a mural tape a long piece of butcher or shelf paper to a long wall. Butcher paper is recommended for younger children. Give the children crayons and see what they come up with. It is important to set ground rules so that the children know that they are to draw on the paper only. Reading a story beforehand can be helpful in getting the children's creative juices flowing. Playing music is also a creative way to enhance this art project. Crayon murals have also been given as large birthday banners to our son's friends. What a pleasant way to let his friends know that they are special. This project is also a great way to entertain children as they arrive at a birthday party!

SANDPAPER CRAYONING

gritty sandpaper (cut into a variety of shapes)
crayons
two pieces of paper
warm iron

Sandpaper crayoning is an art activity that involves using a warm iron. (It is recommended that the ironing be done by the adult for younger children.) Sandpaper crayoning involves cutting very gritty sandpaper into various shapes. The shapes are then colored very darkly with crayons. Place the shapes between two pieces of paper. Press firmly with a very warm iron to set the design. The child will then have a sandpaper picture with sandpaper shapes. We have used this idea turning it into a fall theme. Cut the sandpaper into a variety of different shapes of leaves. Color the sandpaper leaves fall colors and then iron them.

STAINGLASS WINDOWS are another type of art activity that involves the use of a warm iron. There are several types of stainglass windows projects that can be done.

CRAYON AND GLITTER WINDOWS

two sheets of wax paper (cut the same size)
various colored crayon shavings
masking tape
warm iron
aluminum foil covered electric fry pan

Crayon and Glitter windows require two pieces of wax paper cut the same size. The crayons need to be crumbled into small shavings. A hand held food grater works well for this purpose. Some of the crayon shavings and glitter are sprinkled onto the wax paper. The remaining piece of wax paper is then placed on top. The wax paper is then ironed with a warm iron causing the crayons to melt. A frame can be made by putting tape around the raw edges of the wax paper. The frame can be omitted and the cooled window can be traced with a large stencil design and then cut out. This works great with large autumn maple leaves.

Another version of this same project is to place one sheet of the wax paper in a warm aluminum foil covered electric fry pan. The child then sprinkles the crayon shaving and glitter onto the wax paper. The electric fry pan causes the wax to melt and the designs stay where the children originally place them. The sheet is removed from the fry pan and the top sheet of wax paper is then ironed on. Supervision is a must with all of these hot electric appliances in use!

AUTUMN LEAF WINDOW

autumn leaves   warm iron
crayon shavings   masking tape
two sheets of wax paper the same size

Autumn leaf windows can be made by your child and given as a gift to grandparents or someone special during the holiday season. To make an autumn leaf window you will need to go on a leaf hunt with your child. After you have collected a selection of Autumn leaves arrange them on a piece of wax paper. Place Autumn colored crayon shavings around the leaves. Put another piece of wax paper the same size on top of the leaves and crayons. It is now time for the wax paper to be ironed with a warm iron until the crayon shavings have melted. Create a frame by placing masking tape around the raw edges.

CRAYON ETCHINGS

crayons   paper
tempera paint   fork or object used for scratching
brush

Crayon etchings are created by using a three step art process that combines both crayons and tempera paint. To make a crayon etching you will need multicolor crayons, dark tempera paint, paper, and a fork or other object used for scratching off the paint. Have the child cover the paper with a heavy hand in a multicolor design. For best results, a good portion of the paper should be covered with the design. We have found that playing music can help to encourage a more flowing design. The second step involves covering the design with the dark tempera paint. When the paint is slightly dry, etch or scratch the surface with a fork, comb, or other object. This scratching or etching will reveal the colors underneath.

CRAYON RESIST

crayons
watercolors or diluted tempera paints in light colors
paper

Crayon resist is another activity that involves the use of crayons and paint. The paints used in crayon resist, however, are either watercolors or a very diluted tempera paint. To make a crayon resist have your child draw a crayon picture on a piece of construction paper. Brush a colored wash of watercolor or diluted tempera paint over the entire paper. The results are quite striking.

CHALK can also be used as a creative medium for the young child. Some of the more simpler ideas with chalk involve letting the child use white chalk on black paper. This can create a dramatic contrast. Coloring with chalk on large sheets of paper can also be enjoyable. One especially delightful activity with chalk is to let the child draw on the sidewalk with large pieces of chalk. One of my all time favorite chalk activities is called FLOATING DESIGNS.

FLOATING DESIGNS

chalk	bristle block, wire brush or fine grater
grater	shallow container filled with water
plastic knife	paper

Floating designs requires a shallow container or sink, old pieces of chalk (sidewalk chalk works well) a plastic knife or wire brush, and paper. Fill a sink or shallow container half way with water. Use old pieces of chalk and shave them with a wire brush, grater or knife. (Bristle blocks work wonderfully well.) Powder tempera put into a salt shaker with large holes can also be used. Be sure that there is a layer of color floating on the water. Briefly lay the paper on top of the water and lift the design.

LIQUID STARCH AND CHALK

liquid starch in a small container
chalk
paintbrush
construction paper

Liquid starch and chalk is a simple activity that involves painting a piece of paper with liquid starch. Pictures are then drawn on the wet starched paper with pieces of chalk. When the paper is dry, the chalked areas become very brilliant.

CHALK SILLY SHAPES

chalk
pieces of paper
creativity

Chalk silly shapes are created when the child loosely scribbles on a piece of paper. Then with a little creative imagination the child looks for objects, animals, or whatever else he/she can come up with from the scribbles. These objects can then be colored in.

Ideas that worked for me.

Please send us ideas that work for you.

Humanics Learning   PO Box 7400 Atlanta, GA 30357   ·   www.humanicslearning.com

CHAPTER 3
Let's Collage

In the world of early childhood development, a collage is a learning tool that can help children to think about various colors, textures, and forms as they are combined to form a three-dimensional design.

As with all art activities for the young child, there is much to be gained by taking the time to explore the art of collaging. Besides the pleasurable attributes of working with paste and glue this medium also offers opportunities for emotional and aesthetic growth.

To make a collage, a firm base is necessary. Construction paper, meat trays, tree bark, mat boards, and cardboard bolts from fabric stores all lend themselves nicely in the creation of a collage. The surface area should be large enough so that the child has room to work.

In addition to a firm base, paste or glue is also necessary. White glue is the best substance for any surface other than paper. Since we go through large quantities of glue, we now purchase it in a gallon container and fill up our smaller glue bottles or shallow containers when we want to collage. Keep in mind that it is very frustrating trying to glue with glue bottles that are all dried up. Be sure that the glue bottles are in operable condition before you begin your projects. Paint brushes and shallow containers are very helpful for the child who is a little heavy handed with the glue bottles. Q-TIPS can be substituted for the paint brush if spreading the glue is necessary. Homemade paste is fun to make and use with your children. The following recipe is a helpful way to extend the life of your glue.

THINNED WHITE GLUE

1/2 cup white glue
1/2 cup water

Mix the first two ingredients together and put into the container or shallow pan.

The beginner collager can use paste and paper successfully. The following are a few paste recipes that we have found to be useful in the world of collaging. Small pieces of cardboard are useful for putting the paste on when collaging. A popsicle stick can be used as a paste spreader and fingers work great. Keep a moist sponge close by for finger wiping. These recipes for thinned glue and uncooked or cooked paste can be done as a joint effort by both parent and child as an extension to the art experience.

UNCOOKED PASTE

Uncooked paste is a paste that we use when we are down to nothing in the paste jar and still want to do collaging. This is a fast and easy recipe.

1/2 cup water
1/2 cup of flour

Mix the flour with the water. (Be sure to mix in the order given so as to prevent lumps. Paste and have fun!

COOKED PASTE

1 cup flour
1 tsp. salt
2 cups of water

Mix the first two ingredients in a 2 quart saucepan. Add the water slowly be sure to stir until the mixture is cooked. Simmer for about five minutes over a medium to low heat. Cool and refrigerate. A hint of peppermint or vanilla extract can also be added to the paste to increase its aesthetic value.

SHAPE COLLAGE OR GEOMETRIC COLLAGE

variety of shapes and materials (cut randomly or into geometric designs)
glue
collage base

Shape collages or geometric collages are created from a variety of shapes, colors and sizes that have been pasted or glued on a background design. The background paper can be cut into the shape of an autumn leave, turkey, pumpkin, shamrock, or whatever holiday is suitable.

MAGAZINE COLLAGES

magazine pictures
scissors
paste or glue
construction paper

Magazine collages are made from magazine pictures that have been pasted on construction paper. This is a great opportunity for cutting practice. The magazine pictures can be of a particular theme such as people, animals, food, transportation, or whatever interests your child. One of our favorite magazine collage projects was creating our own catalogs using favorite items.

PAPER STRIP COLLAGE

strips of paper (anything goes - the greater the variety the more fun)
collage base (construction paper, tag board or paper plate)
glue

Paper strip collages come to life when a variety of strips of paper are pasted onto a background paper. The strips of paper should be of all varieties of lengths, textures, colors, and patterns. This is an excellent use of old gift wrap, odd sheets of tin foil, and other odd types of papers. Prefolded, fringed and curled ribbons and papers create a dramatic affect. Paper can be cut with a pair pf scissors with the fun edges creating waves or zig-zag edges on your strips.

TORN PAPER COLLAGE

construction paper for base   moist sponge for cleaning fingers
glue or paste   paper to tear

Torn paper collages are a fun activity since the child need only know how to tear. Light weight paper is torn into various sizes and pasted or glued to a background paper. Crayons or felt tip markers can be used to create a dramatic affect once the pasting has been completed. If using markers, be sure the paste or glue is dry first.

IRONED COLLAGE

iron
two sheets of waxpaper (same size)
tissue paper scraps
crayon shavings

Ironed collages are created by the child by placing small pieces of tissue paper and crayon shavings, on a piece of wax paper. Place the other piece of waxpaper on top and have mom iron the design with a medium warm iron until the crayon shavings melt. Glitter or confetti can add interest to this type of collage as well. Contrasting colors such as blue tissue paper with blue and white crayon shavings can create a dramatic design. The finished waxpaper design can be cut into the shape of a dreidel for a Hanukkah theme.

TEXTURED COLLAGES

collage base
glue
textured materials for collaging

Textured collages are great for using up some of the found material objects found around the home. Be sure to use a variety of contrasting textures. One year for Easter we constructed an Easter Basket design. We used a meat tray for the base, a side of a green plastic vegetable basket, Easter grass, a ribbon handle and a piece of fur cut out in the shape of a chick or bunny or a pom - pom ball can be used in the place of the fake fur. Broken up egg shells also are fun to use for the textured collage. Remember the heavier your collaging objects the heavier the background or base needs to be.

FOIL COLLAGE

small pieces of cardboard   glue
scotch tape   small pieces of tissue paper
tin foil

Foil collages are especially delightful during the holidays because of their shiny appearance. Foil collages consist of a small piece of cardboard (about 5x7) covered with tin foil. The tin foil should be taped in place on the back of the cardboard. Brush the foil with glue and place the tissue paper pieces in place. Christmas wreaths are fun to create. For added interest crumble up the tissue before it is glued on.

CLOUD COLLAGE

light blue paper
cotton balls
white tempera paint mixed with a small amount of glue

Cloud collages are constructed from light blue paper, cotton balls, and white paint mixed with a small amount of glue. Have the child paint the light blue paper with the white-paint mixture and add the white cotton balls.

STAINED GLASS WINDOWS

starch   wax paper or construction paper
paint brushes tissue paper

Stained glass windows use wax paper, construction paper, Plexiglas, windows, or tin cans with the paper removed as their collage base. Cut the tissue paper into various sizes and shapes and then place starch moistened pieces of tissue paper onto the desired surface.

DIMENSIONAL COLLAGE

meat trays, box lids or pieces of wood can be used for the collage base
beans, feathers, twigs and shells are great collaging objects

Dimensional collages are created with the use of meat trays for a base and a variety of objects that have been glued to the tray. Box lids, Styrofoam trays, and wood surfaces are interesting collage surfaces for a dimensional collage. The collage material can consist of such objects as dried beans, twigs, leaves, feathers shells or nuts.

DYED RICE COLLAGES

dyed brown rice
glue
firm glue base

Dyed rice collages are a collage construction that are made by combining rice dyed a variety of colors on a collage base. (Food coloring or tempera paint works well. Rice can be placed in a sealed plastic bag with food coloring or tempera. Be sure the rice is dry before collaging.) To create a dyed rice collage spread glue over a piece of paper. The colored rice is then added to the glue to create various designs. For variety glitter or sand can be added to the construction.

YARN COLLAGE

glue
variety of yarn dipped in glue
firm collage base (cardboard works well)

Yarn collages remind us of Autumn and Halloween but this collage can be fun anytime of year. Dip a long piece of yarn in glue and make a free form shape on the collage base. The designs can be a free form shape or they can be made to resemble leaves, pumpkins, hearts, or whatever interests the child.

SMELL COLLAGES

lightweight cardboard or paper plates
glue
variety of spices

Smell collages are constructed from a collage surface that is somewhat firm such as lightweight cardboard or paperplates and interesting smelling spices. It is fun to have the children close their eyes and try to see if they can determine a food that the spice reminds them of. Cinnamon is a favorite collage smell at our house. Try oregano, spearmint, lavender, or other fragrant spices.

FOUND MATERIAL COLLAGE

glue
collage base
anything goes

Found material collage are a fun way to collage with just about anything you can find around the house. We have made found material collages from bread ties, scraps of construction paper, cardboard lids, egg shells and markers for added interest. These objects can be glued onto construction paper.

WOOD SCRAP COLLAGES

wood scraps   tongue depressors
popsicle sticks   generous amounts of glue

Wood scrap collages are made from a variety of wood scraps. These scraps can usually be collected from any place that does any type of wood working. Be sure that the wood scraps are free of nails and rough edges that could cause slivers. Fragrant woods such as cedar and pine are fun to use. Have the child use a larger piece of wood for the base and glue a variety of small wood scraps onto the base. Popsicle sticks and tongue depressors are useful for construction as well as for spreading glue. For this project we usually give generous amounts of glue into small containers. Wood glue works well.

GLUE STAMPING

glue

white paint
objects that can be used for printing such as cookie cutters, an apple cut in half,
a potato, or large number birthday candle

Glue stamping is a fun way to print with white paint mixed with glue. Use any object that will lend itself to printing such as a cookie cutter, an apple (cut in half), a potato (cut in half), or perhaps a large number birthday candle. (A great way to nonchalantly teach number recognition.) Sprinkle the glue with a mixture of sand or cornmeal that has been colored with dry tempera paint. Shake off the excess cornmeal or sand into a tray.

GLUE DESIGNS

glue in glue bottles   glitter
plastic wrap   tempera powder

Glue designs are a wonderful way to let your child have the opportunity to use an abundance of glue. Have the child make a design on plastic wrap. Sprinkle on a generous amount of tempera powder and glitter. Let this mixture dry (depending on the thickness of glue this process usually takes two or so hours to dry.) When the glue is completely dry, peel off the design. A string may be added to create a mobile construction.

GLUE SKIN

glue bottles   child size hand
paint brush   `parent's permission

Glue skin designs are a fun way to give children permission to get glue on themselves. Have the child paint his or her hand completely with glue. Allow this to completely dry. When the glue is dry, have the child peel off the glue skin. This is an especially enjoyable activity for many children.

CARDBOARD BOX GLUING

glue   toilet paper rolls

various size boxes   cylinders

    Cardboard box gluing combines various size boxes, toilet paper rolls, cylinders, and the like to cre-ate three-dimensional collages. Provide ample room and glue. A most enjoyable activity.

FLANNEL BOARDS

large piece of cardboard
flannel large enough to cover cardboard
strong tape such as duct tape
geometric design cut out of felt

Flannel boards are another type of collage activity. Flannel boards are made by attaching a large piece of flannel over a firm piece of cardboard. The ends can be fastened down on the back of the board with durable type tape (duct works great). Geometric shapes and designs can be cut out of felt and can be placed on the board. This is a basic type of collage activity. Stories can also be told with the aid of a flannel board and felt story pieces. Picture books can be easily transformed into flannel board stories. We have even used interfacing colored with magic markers as story pieces. IT LOOKS LIKE SPILT MILK by Charles G. Shaw is a terrific flannel story subject.

The possibilities for collage designs are practically limitless. The following is a list of materials that can be used to make some interesting collages. The gluing base of these collages can be meat trays, tree bark, cardboard, the cardboard bolts from fabric, and mat boards. Most of the following collage materials require glue with the exception of the lightweight paper. The most important thing to remember about collaging is to HAVE FUN!
BARK, FEATHERS, PEBBLES, AND SHELLS
BEADS FROM BROKEN NECKLACES
BEANS OF ALL TYPES

BOTTLE CAPS
BREAD TIES AND PLASTIC BREAD BAG CLIPS
BUTTONS OF VARIOUS SIZES AND COLORS
CARDBOARD BOXES OF ALL SIZES
CELLOPHANE AND NETTING
CLOTH AND WALLPAPER SCRAPS
CORKS OF DIFFERENT SIZES
GLITTER AND CONFETTI
FLOWERS, LEAF, LEAVES, BERRIES, SEEDS, ACORNS, PINECONES,
TWIGS
LEATHER SCRAPS
PAPER OF ALL VARIETIES
RIBBONS, STRINGS,YARN, LACE
ROCK SALT THAT HAS BEEN COLORED WITH A LITTLE FOOD COLORING
SAND OR CORNMEAL COLORED WITH DRY TEMPERA
SMALL TIES
SPONGES ALL SIZES AND TEXTURES
STYROFOAM PACKING
WOOD   SCRAPS,   WOOD   SHAVINGS,   WOOD
C   H   I   P   S

Ideas that worked for me.

Please send us ideas that work for you.

Humanics Learning PO Box 7400 Atlanta, GA 30357 • www.humanicslearning.com

CHAPTER 4
Pleasure With Paints

Most children love to paint and at our house we offer this medium at least once a week. As with all of the activities in this book, the benefits to the child's self-esteem and creative being can not be emphasized enough. There is also a world of learning that is occurring while a young budding artist paints. At first, experimentation with the brush, its strokes, and a single color of paint occupies the child's attention. He/she learns that holding the brush in various ways creates different effects. What an exciting way to learn cause and effect. However, as time goes on and more colors are added, the child learns that combining two colors makes a new color. Quite a discovery for a young child! This is just the beginning!

To have successful painting experiences a few basics are a must.

*Supply the child with ample tempera paint. We have found that red, blue, yellow, black, and white are great basic colors to begin with. With the aid of a little mixing, all the colors of the rainbow can be made. These basic colors also help to keep the costs of art supplies down to a minimum. For variety add liquid starch to the tempera to produce bright and creamy paints.

*Do not skimp when it comes to a good paint brush. It is very frustrating for the painting child to have bristles coming off the brushes onto their pictures or to have the brush fall apart while painting. Teacher supply and craft shops offer brushes with fat handles and wide bristles. We have found this type of brush to be the best for the beginning painter. They are perfect for little hands! We have purchased good brushes for under three dollars.

*In addition to paint, paper is also necessary. Again, teacher supply shops or even the local newspaper or moving companies have newsprint available for sale. The larger the sheets of paper the better. The paper usually comes in large packages and seems to go a long way. For variety, colored paper can be offered or the newsprint can be cut into the shapes of pumpkins, hearts, geometric shapes, or whatever the child desires.

*The type of painting will determine which container will be best for paint presentation. For painting at the table a muffin tin works well if a variety of colors are offered. Juice cans or old yogurt containers work great for easel painting. Encouraging the child to wipe excess paint of the edge of the container will help the paint to go much further.

*Using an old tablecloth or shower curtain underneath the table or area where the painting is to take place is a great aid to clean up. The cloth or curtain can easily be wiped or hosed off when painting time is over.

*At our house a soapy bucket of water and a roll of paper towels are standard fare for painting projects. This is most helpful when it is time to clean those paint covered hands. The paint brushes can also be soaked in the bucket after the child is cleaned up. The disposable paint containers can be thrown away.
*An old short sleeve button down shirt will work nicely as a paint smock. One of dad's or mom's old shirts would be perfect. If long sleeves are used be sure to cut off the excess fabric on the sleeves so they do not end up in the paint. We prefer short sleeve paint smocks with shirtsleeves rolled up.

EASEL PAINTING

easel
paint in disposable cups (be sure they are sturdy so they won't tip)
paint brush
newsprint or large paper

clothespins or masking tape
tarp for the floor
bucket of soapy water

Easel Painting is standard fare at most preschools and kindergartens. This is an activity that is usually eagerly anticipated by young children. Easels can be easily made or purchased at a reasonable price from toy stores, teacher supply houses, or second hand stores. Although this is a piece of equipment that is not essential, it does provide for pleasurable experiences for painting. When we paint at our house, it seems like the children just never get enough. Masking tape or clothes pins work well to hold the paper on the easel. Putting several sheets of paper on the easel at one time really seems to simplify matters as well.

TO DRY PICTURES USE AN OLD CLOTHES RACK OR 3 TO 4 STRINGS HUNG ON A WALL. THE PLASTIC CLOTHES DRYING HOOKS SOLD AT GROVERY STORES WORK GREAT. THESE HOOKS HAVE CLOTHES PINS ATTACHED AND A HANGER AT THE TOP. THESE CAN BE HUNG ANYWHERE. IF YOU ARE FORTUNATE TO LIVE IN A WARM CLIMTATE AND HAVE A CHAIN LINK FENCE, ART WORK CAN BE PINNED ON THE FENCE WITH CLOTHES PINS UNTIL IT IS DRY.

TABLE PAINTING

paper   table top
paint   supplies for clean up
large paint brushes   table top

Table painting is painting without the easel. The paper is placed on the table top and the painting takes place there. Wetting the table with a sponge beforehand will keep the paper from slipping. Large pieces of colored construction paper provides for variety.

GADGET PAINTING

feather dusters
scrub pads
Q-tips
roller

tempera paint (container needs to be
able to accommodate the applicator)
paper
newspaper to cover the painting surface

Gadget painting requires the use of dusters, scrub pads, q-tips, and roller. These materials can be offered at the easel or at the table instead of the paint brush. These materials are intended to be used for painting not printing.

FENCE PAINTING

bucket of water
paint brushes

sidewalk or fence
imagination

Fence painting is the perfect activity for a hot summer day. All that is needed for fence and side-walk painting are one ambitious child, a bucket of water, and a fat paint brush (a clean household paint brush works great). Let the child paint the house, fence, sidewalk, or whatever with the brush and water. This is a very fun and satisfying activity.

WINDOW AND DOOR PAINTING

glass door
paint brushes
tarp or old shower curtain

Window and door painting is an especially fun activity for any holiday season. Sliding glass doors work wonderfully well for this activity. Place a tarp or old shower curtain on the floor and let the child paint on the glass with tempera paint. If a small amount of soap flakes are mixed with the paint, the clean up process becomes even easier. We sometimes display these designs on the door for awhile. Clean up can also be apart of this activity. A large bucket of soapy water and sponges will do the trick.

SEALABLE PLASTIC BAG PAINTING

plastic bag with a seal
two color of tempera paint

Sealable plastic bag painting is a clever way to paint with out any fuss or mess. The child puts several spoonfuls of two colors of tempera paint into a sealable plastic bag. The bag is sealed. The child then guesses what color the paint will turn into. To mix the colors the child gently squeezes the bag. This is an innovative way to help children learn about combining colors. A great paint activity for those who don't like to get their hands messy.

SPONGE PAINTING

wet sponge (cut into small squares)
clothes pin
paint in a shallow container
paper

Sponge painting requires a clothes pin, a wet sponge cut into a small square, paint, and an abundance of paper. Attach a moistened sponge to a clothespin. Dip the sponge into a container of paint. (Meat trays work great as a paint container for this kind of painting.) Sponge painting provides the child with a method of painting that is very different than using a brush. Every child has his or her own style. Some like to dab the paint while others like to wipe the paint on the paper. Sponges precut into a variety of shapes such as the alphabet and animals are now available at craft stores or teacher supply stores The use of the precut sponges add variety to the art of sponge painting.

BLOT PICTURES

squeeze bottle filled with paint
paper folded in half (construction paper works well for this project)

Blot pictures are made by placing tempera paint in squeeze bottles. Old squeeze mustard bottles work well. Be sure to clean them well. The squeeze bottle is especially suited for the younger child. Have the child squirt paint onto a prefolded paper on one side only. The child then folds the paper and presses. Open to see the picture. Older children can use the blot method with brushes and dollops of paint on them. Eye droppers work great too. For added interest and variety the paper can be of various colors and cut into a variety of seasonal shapes such as bats and hearts.

PATTERN PAINTING

plastic or Styrofoam shapes
spray bottle filled with diluted tempera paint
paper

Pattern painting pictures are made by placing plastic or Styrofoam pattern designs onto an absorbent piece of paper. Tempera paint that has been thinned considerably is placed into a spray bottle. The child sprays the paper and designs. Thin pieces of Styrofoam can be cut into the shape of apples, turkey, trees, eggs or pumpkins for holiday themes.

SPLASH PAINTING

| tray | sponge |
| paper | different colors of tempera |

Splash paintings are created by placing a piece of paper on a tray. The paper is moistened with a damp sponge. Drop different colors of tempera on to several areas on the paper and watch the colors run by tilting the tray.

MARBEL PAINTING

box lid or shallow box lined with foil   plastic spoons
marble   paper
disposable bowls filled with tempera paint

Marble paintings require a shallow box or box lid that has been lined with foil. To make a marble painting place a sheet of paper in the box lid. Place several colors of paint into shallow bowl. (Plastic spoons work great for picking up the paint covered marbles.) Have the child drop a marble into each bowl. Place the paper into box and put a paint colored marble on top of the paper. Have the child tilt the box lid and watch the marble create designs across the paper.

BLOWING PICTURES

diluted liquid tempera or small amount of food coloring*
straws cut in half
paper

Blowing pictures can be made with either diluted liquid tempera or small amounts of food coloring. Have the child place a small amount of food coloring or tempera on a nonabsorbent type of paper. With a straw that has been cut in half the colors are blown (it is helpful to have the child practice blowing through straws before they begin their project). For variety white tempera on black creates an interesting affect. (This activity is not suited for twos or younger.)

*Food coloring stains hands, clothes and work surfaces so be sure to protect clothes with smocks, hands with disposable gloves (the kids will love wearing them) and work surfaces with newspaper or a plastic tarp. The colors are vibrant and the kids love this project.

PAINT RESIST

masking tape   paint
cardboard   paintbrush

Paint resist pictures are made by placing strips of masking tape on a piece of cardboard to create a design. The child then paints over the surface. When the paint is dry, the tape is removed to reveal a design.

STRING PAINTING

sheets of folded paper   clothespins
string   tempera paint is a disposable dish

String painting is an especially fun way of painting. To make a string painting the child dips the string or yarn with a clothespin handle into the paint. Place the string on one side of the paper and fold the other side over it. Pull the string out. Open up and see the design.

ROLL - ON - PAINTING

old roll-on deodorant bottles
tempera paint
paper or fabric

Roll - On - painting is a style of painting that uses up your old roll-on deodorant bottles. Remove the plastic tops of the bottles and fill them with slightly thick tempera paint. Replace roll-on tops. Roll paint on paper or fabric. This is a great painting project for twos!

EYE DROPPER PAINTING

old clean eye or medicine droppers
shallow containers filled with tempera paint

Eye dropper painting is a simple method of painting that uses those left over eye-droppers. Children drop paint from the eye-dropper onto a paper. To provide variety for this project try changing the type and color of the paper.

SALT PAINT

equal amounts of flour, salt, water and dry tempera mixed until smooth
paper

Salt paintings are made by mixing equal parts of flour, salt, water, and dry tempera until a smooth and good consistency has been achieved. This paint can also be used in squeeze containers. Salt paint creates a rough texture when it is dry. Applying this medium with a plastic spoon is also an interesting sensation since the child is able to feel and hear the gritty texture of the salt. Sand can also be substituted for the salt.

BALLOON PAINTING

long piece of shelf paper   blown - up balloon
newspaper   large shallow paint container

Balloon painting is an especially enjoyable activity for a small group of children. Place a long piece of shelf paper on the floor (be sure to cover the floor with newspaper first). Blow up a balloon and dip one side of it in a shallow paint dish. To create designs the children gently tap the balloon onto the paper. This is a great outside activity for a summer day!

BUBBLE PAINTING

disposable cup
food coloring or tempera paint and water
straw
paper

Bubble painting combines a small amount of food coloring and water or tempera and water in a disposable cup. Several cups with various colors can be used. The child blows with a straw into the cup until the bubbles are coming out of the cup. Placing a piece of paper on the top of the cup transfers the bubble designs onto the paper.

PRINTING

Paint printing can be a very creative and satisfying activity for the young artist. It is, however, important that the child has had ample opportunity to explore painting with brushes before this medium is introduced. If the child has not had a chance to explore traditional painting before paint printing is introduced, the child may feel the need to use the printing objects as paint brushes. Paint pads can be easily made from meat trays that have a sponge moistened with tempera paint or a paper towel that has been folded and moistened with tempera paint. Printing objects can be as simple as hands, fingers, pencil erasers, cookie cutters, fruits, vegetables, corks, small plastic cars (the wheels dipped in paint and run across paper is a fun activity), or anything that a creative imagination can come up with. For easy clean up use old newspapers placed on the painting surface. As with all art projects, the most important ingredient is to be sure to have fun!

FOOT MURALS

long sheets of shelf paper
pieces of cardboard to be used as paletts
one set of a child's bare feet
bucket of soapy water

Foot murals are created by laying long sheets of shelf paper onto the ground. Pieces of cardboard are used as paint paletts. These paletts are covered with paint. The barefoot child then steps onto the paletts and then walks across the paper. A bucket of soapy water and a towel are a real must. Old tennis shoes also make interesting prints as well.

HAND PRINTING

container of paint   soap and water
a paint brush   a child's hand
paper

Hand printing is one of those activities that is well loved at our house! A container of paint, a brush, paper and soap and water are a must. Have the child paint his/her hands with the paint and then make hand prints on the paper. Another fun project for hand printing is to create a Christmas tree with green hand prints. Several applications of green hand prints are necessary. Don't forget the fingerprint ornaments. We go through lots of paint and paper on this one. This activity is also a great way to keep a record of your child's growth.

TURKEY PRINTS

a child's hand   feathers
tempera paint or washable ink pad   glitter
markers

Turkey prints take hand printing one step further. The child dips his/her hand onto a tempera paint ink pad. (Ink pads are made by placing several sheets of folded paper towel into a shallow container. Paint is then poured on the pad.) Place paint covered hand on a sheet of paper. Add a beak, jowl, leg with markers. Glue can be added to the paint in the paint pad making the addition of feathers and glitters easy.

FINGERPRINTING

containers of paint	fingers
paper	soapy water for clean up

Fingerprinting can be used to produce a multitude of designs. The paint dipped fingers can create letters, flowers, people, animals, or just about anything that the imagination can come up with. Washable ink pads can be substituted for the paint. The child will be able to see all the ridges from his/her fingerprints with this style of printing. The container of soapy water is a real must for this one!

JUICE CAN PRINTING

string that is glued onto one side of a juice can
shallow container of paint
paper

Juice can printing uses string that has been glued onto one side of a juice can. After the string design is dried, the can is then rolled into a shallow container of paint and again rolled onto a piece of paper.

STRING PRINTING

string on a clothespin
shallow container filled with paint
paper

String printing is very similar to STRING PAINTING. The only difference between string painting and printing is in the way that the string is used. This method requires the child to lay the paint covered string on a flat piece of paper creating various designs.

FRUIT AND VEGETABLE PRINTING

paint pad made with a moistened paper towel covered with tempera in a shallow container
variety of fruits and vegetables cut in half
paper

Fruit and vegetable prints are made with a paint pad that is created by folding several sheets of absorbent paper towels and placing this into a shallow container. Cover the paper towel with an adequate amount of tempera paint. (Be sure the paint isn't too thick.) Carrots, celery sticks, apple halves, or potatoes can be used as printing devices. Potatoes that have been cut in half can be cut into designs. This is an activity for the parent. Try pumpkin shapes or leaves. They are just the right size for potato halves.

STYROFOAM PRINTING

Styrofoam shapes cut into a variety of designs
printing pad made with a moistened sponge
paper

Styrofoam printing uses Styrofoam pieces that have been cut and poked into a variety of designs. (Push pins can be inserted into the Styrofoam pieces to act as handles.) Create a printing pad out of a sponge that has been moistened with thick tempera paint that has been placed on a meat tray or paper plate. Commercial holiday shapes can be purchased for printing at arts and craft stores.

CLAY PRINTING

paper
non - water based clay shaped into interesting designs

Clay printing requires non-water based clay that has been shaped by the child into interesting design. Provide a paint pad and paper and presto another printing activity.

CARDBOARD PRINTING

glue   tempera paint
cardboard   paper
paint pad

Cardboard printing is a clever way to glue cardboard into printing shapes. Small cardboard handles can be glued on to aid in printing. For older children large push pins can be used as handles (be sure that the cardboard is thick enough to accommodate the push pin). This activity is especially suited to the older child. This, however, does not exclude the younger child from printing with these designs. Since my child was to young to create his own designs, I created them for him. The printing experience was very satisfying just the same. Use a home made printing pad.

SPONGE PRINTING

sponges cut into various shapes   tempera paint
paint pad   paper

Sponge printing is accomplished by cutting sponges into a variety of shapes. Prepare a meat tray paint pad with desired color paint and print on the paper with the sponge. Interesting scenes can be created with the use of a variety of sponges.

GADGET PRINTING

paint pad
tempera paint
a variety of gadgets to use for printing

Gadget printing is a painting technique that uses any gadget around the house for printing. Prepare a paint pad and collect objects from around the house that would lend themselves to printing. We have used such items as cookie cutters, potato masher, glasses, and pencil erasers. Look for printers that have built in handles for ease of printing. A thick pad of newspaper under the paper to be printed on helps to create clearer results

FISH PRINTS

paint   a fish such as a trout or a carp
paint brush   paper

Fish prints are a reverse printing process since the paint covered fish serves as both the printing object and the paint pad. Lay the fish on a piece of newsprint for easy clean up. Have the child paint on one side of the fish. The prints usually turn out better if an abundance of paint is not used. Place a light-weight piece of paper on the fish and have the child gently rub the entire piece of paper. These prints look very nice mounted on colored pieces of construction paper.

CORK PRINTING

corks   tempera
paint pad   paper

Cork printing uses those old corks from bottles that are normally discarded. Prepare a paint pad with the desired colored paint and have the child use the cork to print with. The end of the cork can be cut flatter for greater ease in printing. Various size corks can be used to create animals such as teddy bears, flowers, or whatever the child's imagination can come up with.

GUM ERASER PRINTS

carved art gum eraser   pencil erasers
washable ink or paint stamping pad paper

Gum eraser prints are created by carving a gum eraser into designs. Carving the gum eraser is a project for mom or dad. Use the carved gum eraser with a paint pad to create interesting designs. Pencil erasers can be used for simple DOT prints.

MONOPRINTING

roller   tray or table
paint   soap
water   sponge

Monoprinting uses a roller to spread the paint on a tray or table. Use a Q-tip or other tool (fingers work great) to make a design. Lift the print by pressing a piece of paper on top of the design.

FINGER-PAINTING

Finger-painting is a most satisfying type of painting for the young child. Most children have a sense of peace and happiness as they paint with their fingers. How wonderful it feels to paint with our body! Better yet, how pleasurable it is to have permission to make a mess.

Finger-painting requires no hidden talents and is an excellent medium for self-expression, exploration, experimentation, imagination, and creativity. This paint medium can have meaning for all ages!

Finger-painting can be accomplished with a few basic supplies.
Traditional glossy finger-painting paper can be costly so we have found ways to minimize the cost.
*One method of finger-painting is to paint right on a table top or a large tray. Clean up is accomplished with a sponge and a bucket of soapy water. The clean up process for many children can be just as pleasurable as the painting. Negative prints can be made by pressing a piece of paper over the paint and gently rubbing.
*Butcher paper is also an inexpensive alternative to finger-painting paper. The slick nonabsorbent side of the paper works wonderful for this activity.
*Shelf paper or newsprint works well as a finger painting paper if 2-3 tablespoons of liquid starch and a generous amount of tempera paint are used.
*A waterproof smock is a real must! The old button down shirt does not serve well for this activity. In a pinch a trash bag smock will work well. As with all plastic products in use around young children, constant supervision is essential. The large toddler bibs that are sold in grocery and department stores work well for finger-painting as well.
*We have found it easier, less expensive, and more enjoyable to create our own fingerpaints. The diversity of creating our own paints also allows us opportunities to work with a greater variety of materials.

SOAP PAINTING

ivory snow   bowl
rotary beater   table top

Soap painting is a variation of finger-painting that uses Ivory Snow that has been whipped with a rotary beater to a light and fluffy consistency. Place a generous portion of the whipped Ivory on the table and let the child have a blast.

STARCH ON PAPER

liquid starch   paper
tempera paint   hands
supplies for clean up

Starch on paper is a great activity for the younger child. The richer and sloppier the paint mixture the better. Pour 2-3 tablespoons of liquid starch on the paper while shaking on a generous amount of tempera paint. For the older child the paint can be poured on the sides of the paper and the child can mix the paint with their hands as desired. Be sure to provide ample paint. Remember a bucket of soapy water and towels for easy clean up.

SHAVING CREAM FINGER-PAINTING

table top or large tray   two ambitious hands
shaving cream   supplies for clean up

Shaving cream finger-painting makes a unique finger-painting medium. A tray or table top and a can of shaving cream are all that is needed. Spray an abundance of shaving cream on the working surface and watch the fun. If you're adventuresome enough, why not join the fun! Clean up is a breeze with soap and water.

PUDDING FINGER-PAINTING

prepared pudding   fingers
table top   mouth for licking up the extra pudding

Pudding finger painting can be a most pleasurable activity. Prepare pudding according to package directions. (We use home made pudding that is easy to prepare and contains all natural ingredients.) Place the pudding on the tray or tabletop and watch what happens. There may be more licking and eating than finger-painting but that is half the fun!

Ideas that worked for me.

Please send us ideas that work for you.

Humanics Learning   PO Box 7400 Atlanta, GA 30357   •   www.humanicslearning.com

CHAPTER 5
A Multitude
of Manipulatives

Manipulative materials are included in this art book because of their value in the area of child development. Materials such as playdough, clay, sand, and mud (to name but a few areas) are beneficial in helping the young child to deal with feelings that are often difficult to express. Pounding on clay or playdough is an excellent outlet for aggressive feelings that are sometimes difficult to verbalize. What a positive outlet for their feelings. In addition to tension relief, manipulatives are also a great way to develop small motor coordination. The child is also given opportunities to pour, sift, stir and measure. Creative opportunities abound with the use of manipulatives.These types of materials can often times be MESSY but children need to have opportunities to make messes. How often we expect children and their surroundings to remain neat and clean. In order to really explore their environments, children should have opportunities to explore without being inhibited. It is important to provides some messy outlets for expression. Working with manipulatives is one such outlet. So be prepared, since next to finger-painting, this is bound to be one of the messiest chapters in this book. There will be opportunities to prepare the manipulative materials together as well as time to explore them. Join in the fun with your child, since all of us can benefit from the FUN!

WATER

water   waterproof smock
container   water toys

Water is so abundantly available but yet we sometimes forget the enjoyable experience that it can provide for the young imagination. Provide a dishpan or some other large container (a baby bathtub works well), a waterproof smock (or a swimsuit if it is a warm day), and some interesting water toys. Funnels, squirt bottles, egg beaters, straws, sponges, basters, eyedroppers, ping- pong balls, ladles, pitchers, measuring cups, tubing, paint brushes, and watering cans can make play more interesting. We have found that adding a few drops of food coloring to the water really adds to the interest level as well. Outside is the best place for water play, but in the winter, however, an old table cloth on the floor or table can do the trick as well. A wading pool outside can be great fun for the child but don't use this method unless you don't mind them jumping in. The temptation not to jump in is just too great. Don't forget the good old bath tub that has been the source of many hours of fun for young children everywhere. As with any water activity,   CONTINUOUS SUPERVISION IS NECESSARY!

SAND PLAY

container for the sand
sterilized sand (can be purchased at major chain toy stores)
sand toys
water
a curious child

Sand is usually a manipulative material that is confined to sandbox play. Since sand feels so good, children usually like to get their entire body involved in the play. This is a versatile manipulative material because it can hold shape once it is wet or it can be poured when it is dry. (SOME SANDS CAN CONTAIN ASPESTUS WHICH CAN BE HARMFUL TO CHILDREN. THE EXCESSIVE DUST CAN BE HARMFUL TO THE LUNGS. IF YOU HAVE SAND THAT IS VERY GRANULAR, HAVE IT CHECKED TO BE SURE THAT IT IS SAFE.) River sand is usually a safe sand for the sandbox. Prebagged sterilized sand can be purchased from large toys stores. Sand can also be purchased from commercial supply companies. These companies are listed in the telephone directory under home improvement or under the heading sand and gravel. If you are unable to house an entire sandbox in your yard, a small container even the size of a dishpan would give the child an opportunity to play with this manipulative material. Some props for sand play that we have found to be enjoyable are dump trucks, bulldozers, funnels, sieves, colanders, scoops, molds, shovels, pails, large spoons, twigs, watering cans (filled with water),rocks, seashells, spatulas, pie tins, plastic animals or any other interesting item that can lend itself to creative sand play. IF SAND IS TO BE STORED IN A CONTAINER OUTSIDE, THEY MUST BE COVERED WHEN NOT IN USE TO PREVENT THEM FROM BEING USED AS NEIGHBORHOOD CAT LITTER BOXES.

MUD PLAY

water	container for the mud (old dishpans)
dirt	soap
buckets	water
shovel	mud clothes
one eager child	

Mud can truly be classified as one of the messiest manipulatives materials and is not intended for the faint hearted. This manipulative is by far the favorite among children. Mud play is one of the least expensive and most abundant material there is. With a little dirt and a lot of water mud becomes endless possibilities. The joyous mud pie is born or with a few buckets and shovels even more creative mud play comes to pass. Unfortunately, our culture is entrenched in the YOU MUST STAY CLEAN model for children. How absurd to expect a young child learning about the world to do it without getting dirty. Dirt and mud are easily removed with a little soap and water so there is no need to deny your young child this pleasure.

In addition to the above mentioned materials, many manipulatives can be made with basic materials found around the home. Each manipulative material project is designed to provide a unique sensory experience. Some of these material are made just by pouring the ingredients into the containers while others require a little more preparation. Have fun and remember messy is a part of manipulative materials.

PUDDING PICTURES

instant pudding (any flavor)   soapy water
wax paper   sponges
hard washable surface

Pudding play can be a very fun activity for the sensorial child. The pudding can be made together by placing the contents in a plastic container with a lid. The child can shake the container until the pudding is of the correct consistency. Place wax paper on a damp table and place pudding on the paper. The child should be given ample opportunity to finger-paint with the pudding. Don't forget to have the child wear a smock to protect their clothing.

SHAVING CREAM or WHIPPING CREAM PLAY

Shaving Cream or Whipping Cream play provides yet another opportunity for the young child to use their fingers in a sensorial fashion. The Shaving cream or the whip cream is sprayed onto a hard surface. The child then is given the opportunity to finger-paint in the material. Younger children find this medium especially satisfying.

RICE AND SALT PLAY

brown or white rice   containers with lids
salt   measuring cups
dishpan

Rice and salt combines to make a very interesting manipulative material. Our friend Sylvia discovered this manipulative. About a cup and a half of brown rice to about 1/2 cup of salt will do the trick. Provide a dishpan or deep container for this activity. This will help to contain the material somewhat better than a shallow container. A sieve will be a most appropriate tool for this material. The child will discover how the rice stays in the sieve while the sand goes through the screen. Containers with lids also seem to be most enjoyable with this activity. Many young children enjoy filling up and dumping out containers.

BEAN PLAY

any large quantity and variety of beans
shallow container
tweezers
jars and measuring cups

Beans of all varieties work well as manipulative materials. THIS ACTIVITY, HOWEVER, MAY NOT BE APPROPRIATE FOR VERY ORAL CHILDREN. For this activity provide your child with a shallow container, a pair of tweezers, and a jar or other type of container. The object of this activity is for the child to place the beans in the jar with the use of the tweezers. This is an excellent activity for building hand-eye coordination in the child. Another bean activity is to have the child practice pouring beans from one container to the other. Yet, another hand-eye coordination building activity.

CORNMEAL PLAY

cornmeal in bulk   spoons
dishpan or other deep container   jars
play objects such as dump trucks   funnels

Cornmeal is a manipulative material that is very much like sand. Cornmeal can be purchased in bulk at some stores. A large bag of cornmeal is fairly inexpensive and will last awhile. We usually play with cornmeal in a dishpan or plastic baby bath tub but any deep container will work well.

CORNMEAL DRAWINGS

cardboard box lid
a small amount of cornmeal
a child's finger

Cornmeal drawings are a home made version of the ETCH-A-SKETCH toy. To make a cornmeal drawing device you will need a cardboard box lid and enough cornmeal to cover the bottom of the box lid. Coloring part of the cornmeal with dry tempera paint can also make for an interesting affect. The child draws designs with his/her finger and when it is time to move on to a new design, gently shaking the box erases the design.

BIRDSEED PLAY

generous amount of birdseed   shovels
deep container for the seeds   funnels
containers (dishpans work great)

Birdseed can be purchased very cheaply at grocery stores. This material can be interesting in that it offers a variety of textures. Toy stores and some educational stores sell water and sand wheels that can be especially fun for playing with seeds, sand, cornmeal, and water. These durable wheels are fairly inexpensive and seem very durable (our wheel has lasted for seven years and is still as good as new). Shovels, funnels, and various size containers will provide for enjoyment with birdseed play as well. The beauty of birdseed is that if it is played with outside, the birds will do the clean up for you.

GOOP

cornstarch   container for the Goop
water   eager child prepared to get messy

Goop ranks up there with mud as far as its messiness. As messy as Goop is, however, it is an often featured manipulative at our home. Goop is made from a two to one ratio of cornstarch to water. We usually start with one cup of water to two cups of cornstarch. The interesting thing about Goop is that is appears to be solid until it is picked up and then it becomes runny. Most children love the sensorial aspect of Goop. Sometimes a few drops of food coloring or dry tempera can be added to the Goop for variety. Spoons, funnels, and small containers are fun to use with this manipulative. We have found that hands are the best prop for Goop. Be forewarned since this project requires many applications of soap and water before clean up is complete. To make clean up a breeze play with Goop outside and hose the area down when play has been completed

PLAYDOUGH

PLAYDOUGH like crayons are synonymous with childhood. There are not many young children that do not enjoy this medium. Like many of the activities already mentioned, playdough also is a satisfying way of relieving aggression. Playdough is easy to get out and easy to supervise. If no playdough is available, it can be made with your child's help in just a matter of minutes. Because playdough is so easy and enjoyable to make there is no reason to ever have to purchase it again. Creativity can be encouraged with the use of several props. Some of the playdough props that are a must at our house are rolling pins (dowels or plastic glasses can work for rolling pins), dull pizza cutters, plastic knives, potato masher, garlic press (fun for making playdough hair), and cookie cutters. Playing with the dough on a large cookie sheet or serving tray is helpful in defining an area of play and helps to keep the dough confined to one place. A plastic shower curtain on the floor helps to make clean up easier.

MISS LEGGETT'S PLAYDOUGH

Some of our favorite playdough was discovered when we were asked to help make playdough for my daughters Heather and Rachael's kindergarten classes with a recipe provided by Miss Leggett.

3 cups flour	3 teaspoons cream of tartar
1 1/2 cups salt	4 tablespoons oil
3 cups of water	food color as you wish

Mix ingredients together. Heat on low heat until the mixture lumps. Stir the mixture into a dough consistency. Store in a plastic bag or an air-tight container. Powdered tempera paint gives the dough a more vibrant color than the food coloring does.

THE WHITE BLOB

1 cup water	1 cup warm water
2 cups Elmer's Glue	2 Tablespoons Twenty Mule Team Borax
	(this can be found at the supermarket)

Mix the 1 cup of water and the Elmer's glue well. In a separate container mix the warm water and Borax. Combine the Borax mixture with the glue mixture using the hands to knead out all the air bubbles. Store in an air-tight container or a plastic zipper bag.

BASIC DOUGH

3 cups of flour	6 tablespoons of oil
1/4 cup salt	dry tempera or food coloring
1 3/4 cups of water (When using food coloring instead of tempera, add it to the water)	

Combine the oil and water and add this to the dry ingredients. Use hands to mix and add more water as needed. This dough will keep well in an air-tight container in the refrigerator for about two weeks.

CLOUD DOUGH

6 cups of flour   powdered tempera
1 cup of oil   light sprinkling of glitter

Mix the flour with the tempera; add enough of the oil to make a soft pliable dough. This dough is very elastic and supple. This dough is greasy so remember to wear smocks and protect floors and carpets. This would be a great dough for outdoors. Store in the refrigerator when not in use.

COOKED DOUGH

2 teaspoons cream of tartar   1/2 cup of salt
1 1/2 cups of flour   1 teaspoon of oil
1 cup of water   food coloring

Combine all ingredients and stir over a low heat for three minutes. Store in an air-tight container or a plastic zipper bag. This dough lasts about a week or so. (This recipe is courtesy of Carol Valentine Gregor.)

COOKED PLAYDOUGH

1/2 cup of flour   1/2 cup of salt
1/2 cup of cornstarch   4-5 cups of flour
1/2 cup of water

Mix the first three ingredients together in the top of a double boiler. Boil 1 1/2 cups of water and 1/2 cup of salt together and pour into the cornstarch-flour mixture. Cook in a double boiler until the ingredients look shiny and translucent.

Stir firmly and constantly. Allow this mixture to cool. Stir in the coloring. Add 4-5 cups of flour until a good consistency has been achieved. This dough is similar to store bought dough. Store in an air-tight container.

BASIC DOUGH TWO

This dough is fun during the holidays when glitter is added to it. This is an elastic and lighter dough.

>3 cups of self-rising flour
>1 cup of salt
>5 tablespoons of alum (this can be purchased at the drug store)
>dry powder tempera

Mix the first three ingredients together along with the dry tempera. Boil 1 3/4 cups of water, add 1/3 cup of oil and pour over the flour mixture. Stir rapidly. Cool and store in an air-tight container when not in use.

CORNSTARCH DOUGH

>1/2 cup of salt
>1/4 cup of cornstarch
>1/3 cup plus 2 tablespoons of water with added food coloring

Mix and cook the salt, cornstarch and water in a double boiler until thick and translucent. The mixture will turn thick and translucent quickly and becomes hard to stir. The extra stirring improves the quality of this dough. Cool to lukewarm on an aluminum pie plate. This is a pretty dough that sparkles and looks almost like gumdrops. A great dough for the winter season.

BAKER'S DOUGH

>4 cups of flour
>1 cup of salt
>1/2 - 1 cup of water

Mix the flour and salt and add enough water to make the dough easy to handle. Let the child knead dough and make into desired shapes. Bake the finished shapes in a 350° oven for about 50 - 60 minutes. This dough makes enough for several children and stores well in an air-tight container in the refrigerator. Finished shapes can be painted with acrylic paint or drawn on with magic markers. (If making ornaments, be sure to make a hole before baking. A nail, knitting needle or straw works well to make the hole.)

ORNAMENTAL CLAY

1/2 cup of cornstarch   2/3 cup of water
1 cups of baking soda

Mix the cornstarch, baking soda and water together and cook in a double boiler or cook the mixture over direct heat - stirring constantly. When the mixture is cool, let the child knead the dough and make into desired shapes. This mixture needs to be used the same day that it is made. A great dough for making ornaments and beads. It is necessary to make holes before baking the shapes. Bake in an oven on the lowest setting until dough appears done. The beads and shapes can be painted or drawn on with magic marker.

FIMO OR SCULPEY CLAY

several blocks of clay   rolling pin
knives for cutting
wax paper
small cookie cutters

Break off two small sections of clay in different colors and have the child work with it by kneading it for several minutes on a piece of wax paper. The more that this clay is worked with the better.   Have the child combine the two colors to create a marble effect. Roll the dough flat with a rolling pin. (Do not use tools from this project for cooking after they have been used on this type of clay). Cut out shapes with small cookie cutters or create beads by placing clay balls on toothpicks on a cookie sheet lined with tin foil. Bake at 275° for 15 -20 minutes. Create all necessary holes before baking. Wash hands thoroughly when done using this clay.

PEANUT BUTTER PLAYDOUGH

2 cups of peanut butter
1/2 to 1 cup of nonfat dry milk
1/4 cup of honey

Mix the above ingredients together. Have the child roll out the dough on wax paper. Let the child use cookie cutters to cut out designs and add chocolate chips, raisins, and coconut for a festive touch. When done don't forget to eat your creation.

Ideas that worked for me.

Please send us ideas that work for you.

Humanics Learning   PO Box 7400 Atlanta, GA 30357   ·   www.humanicslearning.com

CHAPTER 6
Junk Art

Found Materials around the house can be transformed into some very unique art projects. This chapter is devoted to paper bags, plastic trash bags, straws, pipe cleaners, empty boxes, hangers, paper plates, old socks and other interesting items. These items are useful for creating puppets, sculptures, mobiles, masks and even an aquarium. Creating a junk box for collecting these items will help you to be prepared to create some of the projects that follow.

AQUARIUMS

pebbles   liter soda bottle
leaves   water
balloons

Aquariums make use of all those pebbles, small rocks and leaves that we seem to find in our children's pockets all the time. If your child is not one of those avid rock collectors a treasure hunt around the yard or neighborhood can be a delightful way to start the collection of the needed materials for this project. Fill a liter plastic soda bottle (with label removed) about halfway with water. The child then drops his treasures into the bottle. Small balloons that are just slightly blown up and tied at the end represent the fish. They are then placed into the aquarium. Place cap on the bottle. Tape the edge of the bottle top to prevent water leakage. (This project is courtesy of our friend Toshie Honjo in S.D., CA.)

BOWLING

six clean and empty liter soda bottles
ball

Bowling Pins can be made by using six liter soda bottles. The bottles can be decorates with magic marker. Line the pins up and have the children use a ball to bowl down the pins.

TOILET PAPER SHAKERS

flattened toilet paper roll   beans
stapler   magic markers
masking tape   stickers

Music anyone? Toilet paper roll shakers are made by flattening a toilet paper roll. Staple and then tape the end closed with a piece of masking tape. Fill the shaker half way with rice or beans. Tape the end of the shaker shut. Decorate the shakers with paint or magic marker.

TOILET PAPER KAZOOS

toilet paper roll   scissors
hole punch   rubber band
wax paper

This is a great project for those kids who love to sing and hum. To create a kazoo cut a small piece of wax paper and cover the end of the toilet paper roll with it using a rubber band to secure it in place. At the other end of the kazoo a hole is punched with the hole puncher about 1/2 from the edge. The child can cover this with his/her finger for added tone quality. Hum or sing away!

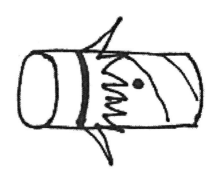

TAMBOURINES

thick paper plates   stickers
hole punch   markers
yarn   jingle bells

    Thicker paper plates can be turned into tambourines. This activity, however will require some help from mom or dad.   Six holes will need to be punched at the same location on both paper plates. With the two bottoms of the plates showing, thread a piece of yarn with a bell through each hole. Tie in place. Decorate the tambourines with stickers, glitter or markers.

STREAMERS

plastic six-pack ring holders   staplers
scissors   streamers

    Streamers are an enjoyable way to help children enjoy music and movement. Take the plastic six-pack ring and cut it into twos. Take one side of the six pack ring cut into two and staple the crepe paper streamers in place. Use the other side as a handle. Turn on the music and let the children enjoy themselves.

LUNCH BAGS aren't just for lunch anymore! Lunch bags are one of those household items that can be used to create an abundance of art activities. We keep a stack on hand just for days when we want something fun to do.

GOODIE BAGS

crayons or markers   lunch bags

Goodie bags are just a simple use for lunch bags. Have your child color the bags with crayons or markers. You can use these bags on walks for collecting treasures on a nature walk. The bags are also useful for collecting peanuts. Peanut hunts are fun. Place the peanuts in the shell around your yard or house and let the child use his goodie bag to collect his peanuts. Goodie bags are also terrific at parties to collect party favors. Why not let each child create their own?

PUMPKINS

lunch bags   paint smock
newspaper   brushes
string   bucket of soapy water
paper towels
small portion of tempera paint (orange and green)

Pumpkins can be made by stuffing a lunch bag 3/4 full with strips of newspaper. Tie near the top with a sting. Paint stuffed portion of the bag with orange tempera paint (this is the pumpkin's body) Paint the top portion green (this is the pumpkin's stem). When the paint is dry if desired draw on a Jack-O-Lantern face with black magic marker.

PAPER BAG WHALES

paper bags	soapy water
newspaper	string or yarn
gray paint	small piece of blue paper
paint brushes	glue

Paper bag whales are similar to the pumpkin in construction. Begin this project by stuffing the bag 3/4 full with small pieces of newsprint. Tie being sure to leave about 1/4 of the bag for the whales tail. Have the child paint the whale either gray or black and white depending on the type of whale your making. Use the wide end of the whale as the head.   Lie the bag on its side and add the eyes, one on each side of the wider part of the bag. Draw a big whale mouth across the bottom of the end. A construction paper water spout can be glued to the whale's back.

BROWN BAG PUPPETS

lunch bag	construction paper
glue	ribbon or yarn
markers	

Brown Bag Puppets are easy and fun to construct. The unopened bag is used as the puppet. The child inserts their hand into the unopened bag and uses his fingers and thumb to operate the puppet. The end of the bag serves as the top of the head, while the mouth can be found under the fold. These puppets can be made into a variety of animals and people.

LUNCH BAG PUPPETS ON A TUBE

lunch bag   construction paper
newspaper   scissors
paper towel tube   magic markers

Lunch bag puppets on a tube are easy and fun to make. The bag is stuffed and decorated with feathers. The bottom of the bag will serve as the top of the head. Hair made out of curled construction paper is fun as well. Don't forget eyelashes, eyes, noses, ears, mouth, and whatever other features are desired. Stuff an empty paper towel roll part way into the bag. Secure with a string. Why not have a puppet show to celebrate your child's creation.

PAPER BAG SNOWMAN

white paper lunch bag
newspaper
staple
scissors

string
buttons
construction paper

Have the child fill the bags with pieces of crumpled newspaper. When the bag is full stapled the top of each bag closed. Tie a piece of sting tightly around the middle of the bag. Let the child glue on buttons and a construction paper hat.

ELEPHANT FINGER PUPPET

finger
scrap of cardboard
(about 5 inches big)

scissors
gray markers

Elephant finger puppets are created by tracing the elephant pattern from the pattern portion of this book. Cutting on cardboard is difficult so this will be a project for mom or dad. Don't forget to cut out the finger hole parents - be sure not to make it too large for the child's finger. Have the child color in their elephant with their favorite colors. When complete have your child insert their finger through the opening. This will be their elephant's trunk.

MOBILES

Mobiles are abstract sculptures that have moveable hanging parts. These parts or forms are suspended in midair by string or yarn that are attached to a main object. Mobile construction have limitless possibilities once you get started. My children love seeing their mobiles hanging from their bedroom ceilings or used as holiday decorations.

HANGER MOBILE

hanger
yarn or string
scissors

nature items
construction paper
nails

A Hanger Mobile can be created by tying a variety of string onto a hanger. (The new colored wire hangers work well for these mobile projects.) The ends of the strings are either tied or glued with a variety of interesting objects. We have made autumn mobiles with sticks, twigs, leaves and the like. We have also made mobiles from construction paper letters with our children's names.

Nails of varying lengths make for an interesting nail mobile as well. If the nails are tied on just right, they will chime in the wind. (AS WITH ALL SHARP OBJECTS, SUPERVISION IS A MUST FOR THE NAIL MOBILE.) Any of the materials that are good for collaging, are usually great for mobiles too.

STRAW MOBILES

straws   small pieces of construction paper
wires   string
lace   yarn
scissors

The child uses straws and wires to construct the base for the mobile. The objects are then hung from the base. There is no set way to make this particular collage. Every child will have their own interpretation. This project gives the child a chance to use creative thinking.

BRANCH MOBILES

tree branches   objects to hang
string   scissors

Branch mobiles are made with the use of a tree branch. A nature walk can be the inspiration needed for this project. Several pieces of string of varying length are tied to the branch. The child can use any item that they choose to hang from the strings. For added interest two branches can be tied together to form an X. String is then tied onto the branches and objects are tied onto the ends of the strings.

PAPER PLATE MOBILES

paper plate   scissors
hole punch   construction paper
string or yarn

Paper plate mobiles can be a fun project and as with the other mobiles the theme ideas are limitless. The paper plate can be turned into a sun and then construction paper stars and moons can be hung on the ends of the string. The paper plate can be decorated with food cut out from a magazine and favorite foods can be glued onto pieces of construction paper and then hung on the ends of the strings. Why not decorate the plate by gluing animals on the plate and then hanging favorite animal glued onto construction paper from the ends of the strings?

HAMMERING ART

large piece of Styrofoam packaging
golf tees
plastic or wooden hammer

Hammering art is a unique way to get rid or Styrofoam packaging from boxes and also to help your child get rid of some of their pent up energy. The child hammers the tees into the Styrofoam to create pleasant designs. Many children just love the idea of hammering. When all the tees have been hammered in, if the Styrofoam isn't too thick, they can be removed by turning the foam over and hammering them out. This is a great hand/eye coordination builder. The best part of this type of hammering activity is that it is quiet.

EGG CARTON TREASURE BOXES

egg cartons   macaroni
tempera paint   tissue paper
pipe cleaner   wall paper scraps
glue   glitter
paint brushes

This is a fun project especially when used for those nature walks. The indentations are perfect for small rocks, pine cones, and the like. To create a treasure box have the child paint the egg carton with tempera paint. (The cartons can be spray painted but this, of course, is a job for mom or dad.) After the cartons are dry a pipe cleaner handle is added. Have the child decorate the treasure box with macaroni, tissue paper, wall paper scraps, and a little glitter. These treasure boxes seem to hold up quite well. (contributed by Jeannie Abshire, San Diego, CA.)

EGG CARTON INSECTS

egg carton   paint brush
tempera paint   pipe cleaners
tape

The inside of the egg carton (the part that holds the eggs) make terrific spiders and caterpillars. To make these creatures separate the top from the bottom of the carton. (Paper cartons work the best.) Turn the bottom of the carton over and cut the cups into either groups of four or a single cup unit. The four cup unit will be the caterpillar's body and the single cup will be the spider. The cups are then painted your favorite insect colors. The bottom of the cups will be the top of the insect. Insert pipe cleaner legs for the spider and antenna for the caterpillar. A multitude of small pipe cleaner legs can be inserted into the body of the caterpillar if desired. Tape on the inside to hold the legs in place.

WEAVING AND STITCHERY

Weaving and stitchery activities besides being enjoyable are an excellent way to build hand/eye coordination. This activity also is useful for the development of small muscle movements in the hand. Weaving will help to strengthen the small muscles that will later be holding pencils and pens to write with. All these benefits to the young child and they only think they are having fun! Sewing projects are especially fun for the young child. With guidance and supervision this can become a favorite activity for the child.

PAPER WEAVING

construction paper strips   scissors
large piece of construction paper

To begin this activity the large piece of construction paper is cut with three parallel cuts across the paper leaving about an inch at each end. The best way to make these cuts is by folding the paper in half lengthwise and then making the cuts. Be sure that the paper strips are about the width of the paper. The weaving motion is an under and over repetition and the reverse on the second row. It will probably be necessary to show your child how to do this motion at first but it won't be long before they are pros.

TOOTHPICK WEAVING

pieces of burlap
colored toothpicks

Toothpick weaving is accomplished by weaving colored toothpicks in and out of such textured fabrics as burlap. This is a great beginning weaving project since there is no wrong way to do it.

SCRIM SQUARES

scrim squares (purchased at Needlepoint shops   masking tape
pipe cleaners, shoe laces or telephone wires   yarn

Scrim squares are another fun and versatile form of weaving and sewing. If scrim squares are hard to find or too costly, onion sacks work just as well. Tape the edges of the scrim squares to prevent unraveling. Weaving can be accomplished with shoe laces, telephone wires, pipe cleaners, blunt needle or a piece of yarn. (If using yarn, dipping the end first in melted wax and letting it harden helps prevents the unraveling that sometimes happens.)

BASKET WEAVING

berry baskets   scissors
yarn or ribbon

Berry basket weaving makes great use of those plastic produce baskets. Yarn or ribbon of various sizes can be used. If using yarn don't forget to dip the end in melted wax or white glue. This will solve that unraveling problem that is so common with yarn projects. Bobby pins also work as good needles too. Weave the yarn in and out of the plastic berry baskets. These baskets can be used for plants or Easter Baskets.

PICTURE FRAMES

old greeting cards   masking tape
hole punch   favorite photo
yarn

Picture frames make great use of those old greeting cards but require a little help from mom or dad to get this project started. Use an old greeting cards cut into the shape of a frame. Holes are then punched around the edges of the frame. The child, using his wax dipped yarn and starting at the top, weaves his/her yarn in and out of the holes. Tie the yarn at the top for a hanger. Tape a favorite photo in the opening.

CEREAL BOX PICTURE FRAMES

fabric squares
glue
buttons
ribbon

raffia
disposable paint brush
old puzzle pieces

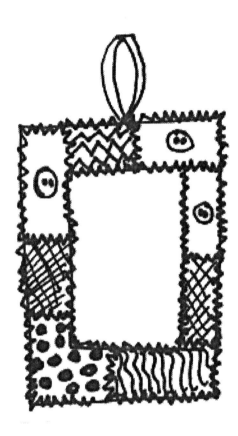

    We have created some terrific holiday gifts with this craft idea. Cut the cereal box into a 5x7 inch frame. Use the paint brush to paint on the glue and then add the fabric strips. To add interest the scraps can be cut with pinking shears. Embellish with buttons, ribbons or raffia. Glue or tape on the back a ribbon hanger or add magnets so that the frame can be hung on the refrigerator. Add a favorite photo by taping it in place with masking tape.

NOODLE FRAME

cereal box   glue
scissors   gold spray paint
variety of noodles

Cut the cereal box into a 5 x 7 frame. Have your child glue on a variety of noodles onto the frame. When the noodles are dry, mom or dad can spray paint the frame in a well ventilated area. The gold gives the frames a rich look. (My daughter's frame still hangs on my refrigerator 6 years later.)

PLASTIC BAG KITES

plastic grocery bags   scissors
permanent magic markers
(remember they stain)

Plastic bag kites are made from plastic grocery bags. Remove the bottom from the bag with the scissors. Have the child decorate the plastic bags with magic markers (remember permanent markers stain clothes). Tie long pieces of string or yarn to the bag. To fly the kite have the child run while holding the kite into the air.

NEWSPAPER SCULPTURES

newspaper   masking tape
large flat piece of cardboard

Newspaper sculptures are an interesting activity for young children. The single sheets of newspaper are rolled into long tubes. The tubes are then attached to the cardboard base with the aid of masking tape. The tubes can be bent and shaped one over the other to form interesting sculptures. The finished sculptures can be painted

CARDBOARD BOX SCULPTURES

cardboard boxes
masking tape

The more variety of boxes used for this project the greater the diversity that the child will have with his/her construction. Have the child tape the boxes together with masking tape to form a cardboard sculpture. This sculpture can also be painted.

LET'S RECYCLE SCULPTURE

cardboard boxes   egg cartons
toilet paper tubes   stickers
plastic bottles   masking tape
bottle and jar lids   film containers

This project utilizes many of the materials found in today's recycle bins. Have the child construct his sculpture using masking tape. In this project one man's trash is truly one child's treasure.

FILM CONTAINER FIRST AID KIT

empty film container   quarter
ribbon   antiseptic wipe
Band-Aid   white blank sticker label
marker

Mini first aid kits are great to have on hand when taking little hikes with the kids. Nothing helps an injury more than a Band-Aid. To create the kit mom or dad will need to punch a hole in the plastic lid. Both ends of a ribbon are inserted into the opening and then tied into a knot. This will be the necklace portion of this activity. Have the child make a label with the child's name and a red cross symbol. Let the child fill the kit with a Band-Aid, quarter for a phone call, and an antiseptic wipe.

GARBAGE CAN CRITTER

green pom-pom   large safety pin
wiggly eyes   3 inch piece of colored tape
tacky glue
film container

The child glues the wiggly eyes on the green pom-pom and then glues the pom-pom into the top of the trash can. Tape the safety pin on to the back of the trash can. Be sure to supervise the young child when they are wearing their garbage can critter.

FILM CAN ROCKETS

film cans
EFFERDENT Denture Cleaner Tablets (about 2-3)
water

This is a fun Science project for the young child. Have the child add two or three EFFERDENT tablets to the film can and add a small amount of water. Replace the lid and place the film can upside down on a hard surface outside. Stand back and watch the rockets blast off into the air.

Ideas that worked for me.

Please send us ideas that work for you.

Humanics Learning PO Box 7400 Atlanta, GA 30357 • www.humanicslearning.com

Chapter 7
Art to Eat

Food can be prepared as an art project for snack time for the young child. Children love having the opportunity to work in the kitchen with their parents and what better way is there for them to learn than to have hands on experience.

My children enjoy helping me prepare meals by cutting, measuring and pouring. At our house little hands tear lettuce into small pieces for salad, grate carrots, cut up vegetable for soup (with supervision) measure and marinate.

Any recipe can be adapted for use by the young child in the kitchen. A rebus card can be created with the recipe by substituting pictures for the amounts and ingredients necessary. This is a wonderful way for children to learn to measure as well as having a hand in their food preparation. Our Peanut Butter Playdough Rebus is a favorite!

I am a firm believer in allowing children to use knives with adult supervision. Dull knives at times can be more dangerous than sharp ones. The children need to be taught how to hold these tools properly and how to properly cut with them. Unless you have the time to supervise and teach butter knives or plastic serrated knives would prove to be a better option.

To help my children so that they can learn to take turns mixing and stirring we sometimes sing "If Your Happy and You Know It" substituting cooking terms and pass it on when it is time to pass it to their siblings. Out favorite line is "If your happy and you know it - stir real hard!" What fun we have.

Messes will occur - that goes with the territory but clean up is also an important part of the cooking process. There are a variety of excellent books on the market devoted to cooking with the young child.

CHEERIOS NECKLACE

CHEERIOS
tape
string

To create a CHEERIOS necklace secure a CHEERIO to the end of a precut piece of string or yarn. Be sure to leave a long enough string for tying when your done.* Putting a piece of tape on the threading end will help to make this job less frustrating for the child. When the desired amount of cereal has been put on the string tie the two ends in a knot. For variety in color and flavor substitute more colorful cereal for this project. SUPERVISION IS REQUIRED WHILE THE CHILD IS WEARING THIS NECKLACE TO PREVENT STRANGULATION!

*The end of the string can also be dipped in melted wax in place of the tape.

ANTS ON A LOG

celery
peanut butter or cream cheese
raisins

Ants on a log are created by having the child clean the celery (be sure to remove the string from the celery to prevent choking). Let the child cut the celery with a knife into 3 to 5 inch pieces. Spread the inside of the log with cream cheese or peanut butter and then top with raisin ants.

CELERY CARS

celery   raisins
carrots   toothpicks
peanut butter

To prepare celery cars have the child clean and cut celery into 3-5 inch pieces. Clean and cut carrots into circles (about 1/4 inch thick-although thicker will be fine). Parents will need to insert two toothpicks through the sides of the celery stick (these will serve as the car's axial. Now it is time for the child to assemble his car. Push carrots circles on the ends of the toothpicks to serve as tires. Load the celery stick with peanut butter and then add the raisin people. (Again supervision is necessary when using such items as toothpicks.)

MR. APPLE HEAD

apples (washed and halved)   plastic knife for spreading
peanut butter   toothpicks
grapes   raisins
cheese cubes

The skin side of the apples are the face. The peanut butter will serve as the hair while the remaining foods will be used to create the eyes, nose and mouth. The toothpicks are used to secure these features in place. Don't forget this project is edible.

HOMEMADE PRETZELS

I package of yeast   1/2 teaspoon sugar
1 1/2 cup of warm water   4 1/2 - 5 cups of flour

Dissolve the package of yeast in the warm water and add the sugar. Add the flour and knead the dough for about 5 - 6 minutes. Let the dough rise in a greased bowl until doubled in size. Be sure to cover while the dough is rising. Divide the dough into pieces and let the child roll them into sticks. The pretzel dough can then be shaped as desired. When finished, blend the egg yolks and water and let the child brush the mixture on the pretzels. Next it is time to sprinkle on some course salt. Place the pretzels on the cookie sheet and bake in a 450 degree oven for about 12 minutes.

PRETZEL SCULPTURES

stick pretzels
peanut butter playdough

Set out the pretzels and playdough. Have the children roll the peanut butter playdough into balls. To create sculptures the child sticks the ends of the pretzels into the balls of playdough.

MARSHMALLOW SCULPTURES

miniature marshmallows
toothpicks

To create marshmallow sculptures have the child insert the toothpicks into the marshmallows being certain that both ends of the toothpicks are covered. Have the child continue to build his creation until he has used as many marshmallows and toothpicks as necessary. Be certain to supervise this activity since toothpicks can be sharp.

MR. POTATO HEAD

Baked Russet Potato   broccoli
cheese cubes   cheese cubes
toothpicks   pickles

Prebake and cool the potato. If time warrants, you can give the child an opportunity to help cut and cube the vegetables. The vegetables and cheese cubes are then attached with toothpicks to serve as Mr. Potato Head's features. Sour cream can be used as the glue to help attach the vegetables. When done be sure to eat and enjoy!

SPACE SHIPS

half of a banana   pineapple slice
cherry   lettuce leave

The lettuce leave will serve as the launching pad. The pineapple slice is then placed on top of the launching pad. The half banana is then placed into the pineapple slice. A cherry is the nosecone and can be secured in place with some whip cream.

MR. PIZZA FACE

English muffins   olives
spaghetti sauce   mushrooms
cheese   pepperoni, ham, ground turkey or beef

Half of the English Muffin will serve as Mr. Pizza's face. Put on sauce then top with cheese. Decorate the face with features using the remaining foods. Bake at 350 degree oven until the cheese melts.

PEANUT BUTTER PLAYDOUGH

2 cups of peanut butter
1/2 to 1 cup of nonfat dry milk powder
1/4 cup of honey

Mix the following ingredients together. Sunflower seeds, raisins, coconut, chocolate chips or granola can be used to embellish the dough. It is fun to make designs with cookie cutters, add the above mentioned goodies and then, of course, eat the creation when it is finished.

PUDDING FINGER PAINTING

1 package of pudding mix
milk
mixing bowl with lid

Combine milk and pudding mix in the container. Place the lid on the container and have your child shake vigorously until the pudding is of the correct consistency. Place several spoonfuls of pudding on a clean cookie sheet, tray or wax paper. Let the child finger paint. This activity is especially suited to the toddler who loves to play with and experience his/her food.

CRITTER TOAST

toast	jelly
peanut butter or cream cheese	knife

To create critter toast the bread is first toasted. Decide on what type of critter design your child would like. Cut the toast in triangles, squares or circles. Cookie cutters are a fun way to shape toast into various critters. Some of our favorite critters are butterflies, elephants, rabbits, and happy faces.

SANDWICH CUT OUTS

peanut butter	bread
jelly	cookie cutters

Use cookie cutters to cut out the design on slices of bread. Spread on peanut butter and jelly. We have made pumpkin shaped sandwiches for one Halloween that were a huge success.

POPSICLES

juice
paper cups
popsicle sticks

The child pours juice into cups and then adds sticks. Put in the freezer and check occasionally to see the changes in the juice. Fruit flavored yogurt can be added to the mixture for added interest.

SHISKABOBS

watermelon cubes   banana chunks
cantaloupe cubes   strawberries
wooden skewers

The child arranges the fruit pieces on the skewers according to his/her design. (Supervision is needed during this projects - skewers can be sharp.) Children can also assist with the preparation of the fruit by helping to cut it up.

SMOOTHIES

bananas   egg
fruit juice (apple works well)   1 tablespoon of peanut butter
frozen strawberries   handful of almonds
a few seeded dates   extra juice as needed

The child puts all the contents into the blender in the order given. Pour enough juice to blend. Let the child push the blend button until the contents are mixed. The mixture should be of a thick consistency. Place in a fancy glass with straw, coconut and a strawberry on top.

SNOWMEN

two mini rice cakes   raisins
cream cheese   celery sticks
 (flavored cream cheese can be used)

Have the child place the two cakes on a plate and cover them with cream cheese. Add two celery sticks for arms, a raisin face and raisins for buttons.

BUTTERFLIES

hard boiled egg - sliced in half   cream cheese
slice of bread cut into a triangle   sliced olives
thin carrot sticks

The child places one half of the hard boiled egg yolk-side down on the plate. The bread is then spread with cream cheese and positioned point side of the triangle toward the egg. These represent the butterfly's wings. Place sliced olives on the cream cheese for pattern on the wings. Celery sticks serve as the antenna.

EGG SALAD

hard boiled eggs in their shells
mayonnaise
crackers

Give the child the opportunity to peel the hard boiled egg. After the eggs are peeled let the child mash the eggs with a potato masher. Add a small amount of mayonnaise and pepper. When the mixture is complete it is time to spread on crackers or rice cakes.

POPCORN COLLAGE

popcorn
light weight cardboard (old cereal boxes work well)
glue

Pop some popcorn with your child. Although the microwave and air poppers are fun and a healthier way of preparing popcorn I sometimes use the old fashion method of heating oil in the pan. Place the kernels in the hot oil in the pan and place the lid on, listen to the sound of the pop, pop, popping on the metal lids. It is music to our ears and sometimes we even sing songs or make up poems. Don't forget those delicious spices and butter but be sure to reserve some plain popcorn for your art project. We have on occasion written my son's name on a piece of cardboard and then glued the pieces of popcorn over his name. This portion of the project is not edible.

WALNUT BOATS

walnuts   buttons
toothpicks   glue
pieces of white paper

The child with the help of mom or dad crack open the walnuts. After the snack of walnuts the shells are used to make boats. A toothpick if glued into the bottom half of a walnut shell. (Low temp glue guns really come in handy for this—again supervision is an absolute necessity.) Cut a small triangle of white paper and use this for the boats sail. These boats can be placed in a tub of water and the child can blow like the wind and watch the boat travel.

Chapter 8
Seasonal Art

It can be a child's delight to help in the creation of holiday decorations, cards and gifts. My children derive a great sense of pleasure being able to decorate for the holidays with the different projects that they have done through the years. These decorations have become precious keepsakes. Almost all of the projects in this book can be adapted for a holiday theme by using the appropriate colors associated with that holiday.

HALLOWEEN

PAPER PLATE MASKS

paper plates	sequins
scissors	beads
white glue	yarn
feathers	scraps of paper
popsicle stick	masking tape
markers	

Paper plate masks have unlimited possibilities. The plates can become characters in a favorite story or a favorite animal simply by embellishing the bottoms of the plates with any of the above mentioned supplies using white glue. Don't forget to cut eye holes. A handle is added by taping on a popsicle stick.

GHOSTS

paper dinner napkin
black pipe cleaner
glue

wiggly eyes
black magic markers

Ghosts can be created by opening up a white dinner napkin and placing another napkin rolled up into a ball into the center of the napkin. Close up the napkin with the ball in the center and tie it off with a pipe cleaner. Glue on wiggly eyes and use the marker to draw on a mouth.

TOOTSIE POP GHOSTS

TOOTSIE POPS
napkins
ribbons

TOOTSIE POP ghosts are created by placing a lollipop in a dinner napkin that has been completely opened up. Tie a ribbon on the outside where the lollipop and stick meet. Pipe cleaners can be used in the place of the ribbon if desired.

BAT BLOTS

black paper folded in half and cut into the shape of a bat
eye droppers or medicine droppers
acrylic paint in a disposable container (tuna cans or yogurt cups work well
with a paint brush)
or a squirt bottle filled with acrylic paint

Dabs of acrylic paint are placed on only one of the insides of the bat wings. Use any of the above mentioned methods for applying the paint. The paper is folded in half and then rubbed on the outside. The impression is transferred onto the opposite side of the bat's wing. Be sure to have several bats available because one is never enough.

PAPER BAG PUMPKINS

lunch bags   orange acrylic paint
newspaper   paint brush
yarn   paint smock

Paper bag pumpkins are a Halloween tradition at our house. It is very satisfying for the children to be able to tear newspaper, roll it in a ball and then place it into the lunch bag. Fill lunch bag 3/4 full and tie near the top with yarn. Paint the stuffed portion of the bag with orange paint. When paint is dry add Jack-O-Lantern features with black magic marker.

WINDSOCKS

construction paper   string
streamers   hole punch
staplers   glue
markers

Windsocks are created by having the child create a design on the paper. (The paper should be vertical. Big orange pumpkins can be created out of orange construction paper or even bats can be glued on. A simple ghost can be created by using a white piece of construction paper and having the child add big black eyes either with construction paper or with marker. Five or six streamers about 24 inches long are then glued to the bottom edge of the construction paper (be sure to glue the streamers on the back of the paper). The paper is then rolled into a cylinder and stapled. Two holes are then punched into the top and a piece of string is tied into place as a hanger. Hang in the wind and watch your sock fly!

PUMPKIN NECKLACES

walnuts   paint brushes (large and small)
orange paint   green felt
black paint   scissors
1/4 inch green ribbon-necklace length

Have the children paint the walnuts orange and let dry. A pumpkin face is then painted on the walnut and allowed to dry. Cut small pieces of green felt into a leaf shape for the top of the pumpkin - place ribbon under felt piece and glue to the top of the walnut. Low temperature glue guns work well for this project.

HALLOWEEN CAT

2 pieces of black construction paper   scissors
yellow construction paper   white pencil
stapler   glue or glue stick

Using the cat and spiral pattern in the pattern section of this book the parent should trace the shape of a cat and spiral onto the black pieces of construction paper. The older child can cut the cat, circle and spiral out themselves while the younger child should have the cat and circle precut. The parent then should draw the spiral pattern onto the circle. The child then practices their cutting skills by cutting the lines on the spiral until they reach the center of the circle stopping at the x. I sometimes hold the circle and turn as the younger child cuts. Cat eyes, whiskers, a nose and a mouth are then added to the cat's face. The tail (previously a spiral) is then stapled onto the bottom of the paper.

SPIDER

black construction paper precut into 8 2 inch strips
black construction paper cut into the shape of a spiders body
glue or glue stick
scrap paper for eyes
scissors

It is best to start by adding the eyes to the spiders head. Glue pieces of white or yellow construction paper on for the eyes. If the child is old enough, have them practice accordion folding the black construction paper strips. If this task is to difficult have them skip this step and then glue the spider legs onto the body. Don't forget four legs on each side!

STYROFOAM BALL SPIDERS

Styrofoam oval ball - about 3 or 4 inches
4 black pipe cleaners - cut in half
wiggly eyes
glue

The eyes are glued on to the narrow end of the oval ball. The pipe cleaners are then inserted into the sides of the ball remembering to place four on each side. Don't forget to bend the legs to make it look like the spider is walking.

THANKSGIVING

TURKEY HAND PRINT

hands
variety of acrylic paints
paint brush
paper towels
red and black markers or crayon

construction paper
feathers
glitter
soapy water

Turkey hand prints are a favorite and treasured art project in our home, Help the child by painting their hands with acrylic paint. We paint the palm and thumb one color and the rest of the finger different colors. The hand print is then transferred onto a sheet of construction paper. While the paint is still wet let the child add glitter and feathers to the fingers. After the turkey is dry don't forget to add the eyes, feet and, of course, the turkey's jowl.

PAPER PLATE TURKEY

autumn color construction paper   scissors
glue   paper fastener
crayons

Have the child color the paper plate brown. Cut about 6-8 narrow strips of construction paper in various colors that are each about 6 inches long. These strips will serve as the turkey's feathers. Have the child glue the feathers so than only about 3 or 4 inches are hanging over the edge of the top of the paper plate. A turkey head is created out of brown construction paper (an elongated pear shape works well for the head and neck). Draw on eyes, glue or draw on a beak and a jowl. The neck is then attached with a paper fastener at the bottom of the plate. Don't forget to create construction paper feet and then glue them on.

Another version of the paper plate turkey involves making 6-8 cuts 3-4 inches long on top of the plate.   These   serve   as   the   turkey's   feathers.   Have   the   child   color   various
c   o   l   o   r   s   .

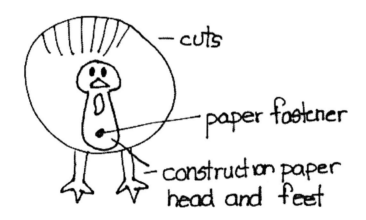

PINE CONE TURKEY

pine cones (try to find ones that are able to stand up on their ends)
feathers
pipe cleaners - use a thick brown one
glue

A treasure hunt to find pine cones is a great beginning for this project. After locating pine cones wrap the pipe cleaner around the smaller end shaping it to look like a turkey's head. Add feathers (dip the end in white glue or tacky glue) and slip in between the crevasses at the end of the cone. (Pine cones can be painted with acrylic paint and then glitter can be sprinkled on the pine cone before the turkey's head and feathers are added.)

CHRISTMAS

PAPER CHAINS

construction paper scraps
markers
25 construction paper strips (2x8) various colors
tape, glue or stapler

Paper chains are a fun way to count the days to Christmas. Have your child create a paper chain by taping, gluing or stapling the strips together by using red and white or green and red paper. The final chain should have a Christmas Tree, Santa or a favorite holiday symbol representing Christmas day. One chain is removed each evening before bed until the last chain remains. Paper chains have become a tradition in out house. We also use paper chains to help us count the days of Hanukkah. This helps us to remember how many candles to put into the menorah.

FIRECRACKERS

toilet paper rolls
several pieces of candy
small inexpensive toys (small enough to fit into the tube)
small rectangular pieces of gift wrap
scotch tape
6 inch pieces of curling ribbon.

These are fun and easy craft projects that are also great for gift giving. (Placing firecrackers around the dinner table can be a fun way for the children to make a festive contribution to the Christmas dinner.) It is really helpful to have the materials precut for this project. Have the child stuff the toilet paper tubes with a few pieces of candy and a small toy. Wrap the paper around the tube and tape in place. Tie the ends Tootsie Roll fashion.

PAPER PLATE SANTA CLAUS

paper plate   construction paper (red, white, blue)
glue   cotton balls
scissors

To create Jolly Old Santa Claus create a stocking hat by cutting a triangle that is as wide as the paper plate. Glue the stocking hat onto the top of the paper plate. Add white cotton balls for border on the hat and add one of the cotton balls as a pom-pom at the tip of the triangle. Add eyes and a nose either with marker or pieces of construction paper. Don't forget to give Santa his mustache with either a piece of white construction paper or a cotton ball.

TOILET PAPER ROLL REINDEER

toilet paper roll   small pieces of ribbon
2 small twigs   brown acrylic paint
small pieces of masking tape   paint brush
small circles of construction paper (a hole punch works great)

Make four one inch rectangules on the bottom of the tube with black marker. These will be the reindeer's feet. Paint the tube with brown acrylic paint. When the tube is dry, glue on eyes, nose and mouth using hole punch paper. Punch two holes at the top of the tube. Place a small twig one in each hole and tape them in place from the inside.   For a finishing touch glue on a small ribbon under the reindeers face.

hole punch

GIFT WRAP

tissue paper or butcher paper
stamp pads
stamps

Home made gift wrap is fun and easy to make. To make the paper have the child stamp designs all over the tissue paper or butcher paper. For a fun variation cookie cutters can be used with acrylic paint. To make an acrylic paint pad use a moistened paper towel covered with the paint. Use the cookie cutters as stamps. For a more natural look brown paper can be stamped with leaf prints and then tied with raffia. Pine cones and leaves are a terrific addition.

CARDS

construction paper or any paper   doilies
glue   ribbons
fancy scissors and a regular pair   sequins
markers   glitter

Fold card into desired size. Use the fancy scissors to decorate edges. Embellish cards with ribbons, doilies, sequins, markers and glitter. Have the child write their sentiments or let the younger child dictate their messages and sign their names. (To create a pop up card have the child cut an object such as a Christmas tree out of construction paper. Fold it in half. Open the card and then have the child just glue the edges of the tree down right over the fold of the card lining up the inside of the cards fold with the trees fold. When dry the tree will pop up when the card is opened.) The possibilities for this project are limitless.

PAPER PLATE WREATH

paper plate   ribbon
scissors   glue
tissue paper squares (red, green and white)

A little preparation is necessary before beginning this project. The center of the plate needs to be removed leaving a rim about 3 inches wide. The tissue paper squares should be cut into about three inch squares. To create a paper plate wreath have the child glue pieces of tissue paper onto the paper plate rim. For a fuller look twist the tissue paper on the end of a pencil and then dip the end into the glue. The tissue paper is then added to the wreath.

FOOTPRINT ANGEL

one foot   scissors
one set of hands   glue
white and a light colored piece of paper
markers
pipe cleaner

To create an angel trace the child's foot on the white paper. Trace the child's hands on the lighter piece of paper. Cut out the shape of the foot and the hands. Place the foot with the heal up and then glue the hand shapes one on each side of the foot in the middle by the arch. The hands will serve as the angel's wings. The heal of the foot will serve as the angel's head so draw in the features and don't forget to glue on the pipe cleaner hallow.

HANUKKAH

MENORAH

clay (FEMO OR SCULPY works great)
9 washers (make sure that the candles fit into the washers)
birthday or Hanukkah candles

Have the child form the clay into a design about 5 inches long and about 1 inch wide and about 1/2 inch thick. The nine washers are then pushed down into the clay. The washers will serve as the candle holders. In a real menorah one of the candles (the Shamus- the helper candle) is higher than the other candles. To create this affect the center of the menorah can have an extra piece of clay added before the washer is put into place. The menorah is then baked on a foil covered tray in a preheated 275 degree oven. Allow to cool as the washers will be hot. Be sure to have the child wash their hands well.

PAPER PLATE DOVE

paper plates   paper fasteners
scissors   markers

The dove is a symbol of peace for all people. To create a paper plate dove use the pattern located in the pattern section at the end of this book. The dove is created by cutting two paper plates to form the body and the wing of the bird. A hole is made using a hole punch at the top of the wing and on the birds breast. The wing is then attached with a paper fastener. Markers are then used to decorate the bird.

HANUKKAH GIFT WRAP

Hanukkah cookie cutters
yellow and blue acrylic paint
soapy water for clean up

butcher paper
paper towel
Styrofoam tray

Hanukkah gift wrap is fun to create with the use of butcher paper, cookie cutters and a Styrofoam foam stamp pad. The stamp pad is created by moistening a paper towel and spreading a layer of acrylic paint on it. The cookie cutter is then dipped into the paint and stamped onto the butcher paper. Easel painting pictures also make terrific gift wrap.

STARS OF DAVID DECORATION

6 popsicle or craft sticks
glue or low temperature glue gun
acrylic paint
glitter

The popsicle sticks are glued together to form two separate triangles. If using white or tacky glue, allow the triangles to dry well before proceeding onto the next step. The triangles are then layered on top of each other one pointing up the other pointing down. They are then glued together. When the glue is dry the child can paint the Star of David and add glitter. Be sure to sprinkle the glitter while the paint is wet and over a piece of paper. Glitter is fun but messy. A picture of the child can be taped to the center back of the Star of David transforming this project into a picture frame suitable for gift giving.

DREIDEL COLLAGE

strips of colorful paper (use gold, yellow, whites and blue)
strips of tin foil
pieces of Hanukkah gift wrap
glue
solid piece of paper for dreidel any favorite Hanukkah color will do
Hanukkah stickers
curling ribbons about 6 inches long

Trace and cut out the dreidel using the pattern found in the pattern section of this book. The dreidel shape is then decorated with the various materials listed above using glue to hold them in place.

STAIN GLASS DREIDEL

wax paper   crayons - blue, white, yellow
scissors   stars
blue, gold or silver glitter   cheese grater
iron   ironing board
newspaper

Cut two pieces of wax paper about the same size. Remove the wrapper from the crayons. The child then grates the crayons using the small holes of the grater over one of the pieces of wax paper. Use several colors of the crayons. Add glitter and stars. The second sheet of wax paper is then placed on top. The two pieces of paper are then transferred to the newspaper which is placed on top of the ironing board. The ironing portion of this project should be done by the adult. The crayon shavings are melted by rubbing a hot iron over the surface of the wax paper. When the paper cools, the dreidel shape from the pattern section of this book is then traced onto the wax paper and then cut out. Place the stain glass dreidel in the window to appreciate its beauty.

EASTER

BUNNY BAGS

lunch bag
stapler
2 pink pom-pom
wiggly eyes

Easter Grass
glue
Easter treats
white floral wire

Bunny bags are fun to create during Easter. Be sure to use the bunny bag pattern found in the back of this book in the pattern section. Trace the pattern on the bag and cut out the bunny ears. Glue on the wiggly bunny eyes. Cut the white floral wire into three six inch pieces. Glue the floral wire under the eyes and then add the bunny's pom-pom nose. Don't forget the bunny's mouth. When the face is complete, staple the two remaining pieces (they look like ears and are on the back of the bag) together. Be sure to glue a pom-pom on the back of the bag for the tail.

EASTER BASKETS

green berry basket
ribbon (1/4 inch wide)
two large yellow pom-poms

glue
small piece of orange paper
Easter grass

This project will give the child a chance to weave. Cut pieces of ribbon and have the child weave them in and out of the openings in the berry baskets. When the child finishes one color, and wants to go on to the next, have them tuck their ends into the last hole on the inside of the basket. When the weaving is complete fill the basket with the grass. Add a pom-pom chick to the basket by gluing the two pom-poms together and add a tiny orange triangle beak. Place the pom-pom chick in the basket. (Bobby pins work great as needles.)

MOTHER'S AND FATHER'S DAY

HAND PRINTS

hands   paint brush
acrylic paint   soapy water
tag board (about 8' x 11")   paper
photo of your child   poem listed below

One of my favorite gifts from my children have been their hand prints with their photos attached. To create these precious gifts paint the child's hands and make a set of hand prints on the tag board. Leave a section of tag board in between the hands open so that the poem can be inserted. Cut out a favorite photo of your child and glue at the top above the hand prints. Don't forget to place the date or the age of your child.

You always clean my fingerprints
I leave upon the wall
I seem to make a mess of things
Because I am so small

The years will pass so quickly
I'll soon be grown like you
And all my fingerprints
Will surely fade from view.

So here's a special hand print
And a picture of me too
So you'll recall the day
I made it just for you!
Author Unknown

HUGS

butcher paper   one set of child's arms
markers   scissors

Hugs are terrific for mother or father's day or to send to grandparents who live far away. Have the child lie down on the butcher paper with their arms extended. Mom or dad need to trace both outstretched arms as far into the torso as possible. Have the child get up and then connect the arms in the middle. Label the arms saying THIS IS A HUG FROM and then your child's name. Be sure to have the child decorate the hug. Cut out the arms and hands. Take the hug and wrap it around yourself and get a great big hug.

ST. PATRICK'S DAY

ST. PATRICK'S DAY COLLAGE

green construction paper   glue
stickers   scissors
green things such as: buttons, green noodles, green feathers, split peas or stickers

Draw a shamrock on the green paper and then cut out. (A shamrock pattern is located in the back of the book in the pattern section.) Have the child glue a variety or green objects onto the shamrock. Don't forget the gold glitter.

VALENTINE'S DAY

CINNAMON SCENTS

1 cup of cinnamon   3/4 cup of applesauce
1 tablespoon cloves   2 tablespoons of White Elmer's Glue
1 tablespoon nutmeg   wax paper

Mix dry ingredients and then add the wet ingredients. Roll out the dough on a wax paper surface that has been sprinkled with cinnamon. Cut the dough into shapes such as hearts with small cookie cutters. Remember to create a hole with a nail or straw if these creations are to be hung up. Let the creations dry for 2 to 3 days. Be sure to turn a couple of times. (Courtesy of Michelle Steinberg)

Chapter 9
Let's Dress Up

Young children love to dress up and pretend. This is referred to as dramatic play. Our son was forever wanting to wear daddy's big shirts and shoes. This section Let's Dress Up will also give the child another avenue in which to express him or herself. It is interesting to watch and listen to our children as they dress up and pretend. Listen closely and you may even hear yourself speak through your child or see your mannerism mimicked.

Many dramatic play props can be made by both parent and child. These props will help to enhance and encourage this type of play. Our play room has a special section of home made dress up materials. These are well loved and remade and replaced as needed.

CHEERIOS NECKLACE

CHEERIOS
tape
string

To create a CHEERIOS necklace secure a CHEERIO to the end of a precut piece of string or yarn. Be sure to leave a long enough string for tying when your done. Putting a piece of tape on the threading end will help to make this job less frustrating for the child. When the desired amount of cereal has been put on the string tie the two ends in a knot. For variety in color and flavor substitute more colorful cereal for this project. SUPERVISION IS REQUIRED WHILE THE CHILD IS WEARING THIS NECKLACE TO PREVENT STRANGULATION!

NOODLE NECKLACES AND BRACELETS

string or thin elastic   noodles
rubbing alcohol   ZIPLOCK bag
food coloring

  Noodle necklaces and bracelets are made by having the child string the noodles onto a string or a piece of thin elastic. Tying the end of the string with one of the noodles will keep the rest of the noodles on the necklace. When the desired amount of noodles are on the string, the two ends of the string are then tied together. For added interest the noodles can be colored beforehand. To color the noodles, mix a small amount of rubbing alcohol and food dye in a Ziplock bag. Place noodles in a bag and shake. After the noodles are the desired color lie on a paper towel or newspaper to dry. Try a variety of noodles for your jewelry creations.

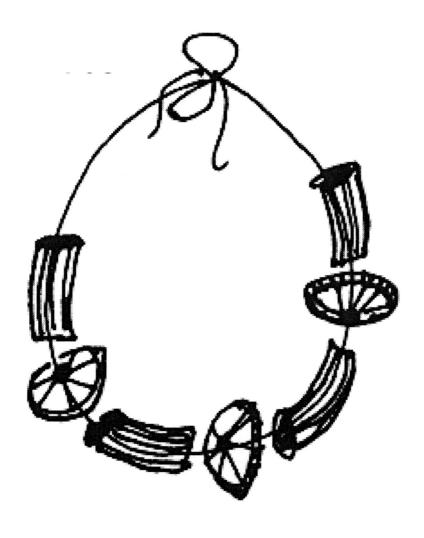

JUICE CAN LID NECKLACES

juice can lid (frozen variety)
stickers or photos
glue
ribbon

Juice can lid necklaces are made by decorating the lid of a frozen juice can with stickers or by gluing on a favorite photo. Measure a piece of ribbon long enough to go around the child's neck and then tape the middle of the ribbon onto the back of the lid.

FIMO OR SCULPEY CLAY JEWELRY

several blocks of clay   rolling pin
knives for cutting   wax paper
small cookie cutters

Break off two small section of clay in different colors and have the child work with it by kneading it for several minutes on a piece of wax paper. The more that this clay is worked with the better.   Have the child combine the two colors to create a marble effect. Roll the dough flat with a rolling pin. (Do not use tools from this project for cooking after they have been used on this type of clay.) Cut out shapes with small cookie cutters or create beads by placing clay balls on toothpicks on a cookie sheet lined with tin foil. Bake at 275 degrees for 15-20 minutes. Create all necessary holes before baking. Wash hands thoroughly when done using this clay.

HAIR AND WIGS

brown paper grocery bag
markers or acrylic paint (your favorite hair colors)
scissors

Paper bag wigs are a great way to create a new head of hair for those bag hair days. To create a wig have your child draw a hair line onto the paper sack. The child then cuts on the outline of the wig. The sack is then painted the desired hair color. Curls can be created by cutting the bag into strips and then curled with the edge of the scissors. Magic markers can be used for highlights.

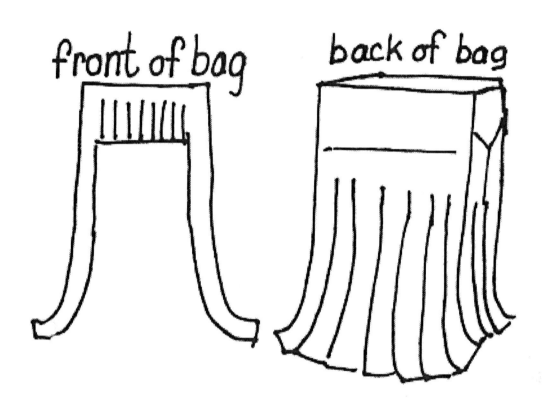

MUSTACHES AND BEARDS

scissors
construction paper
scotch tape

Short on facial hair? Why not create your own mustache. This easy project requires cutting a piece of construction paper (your favorite hair color) into a mustache shape. Be sure to leave a small indentation to go around the nose area. A piece of scotch tape folded back on itself can help keep the facial hair in place.

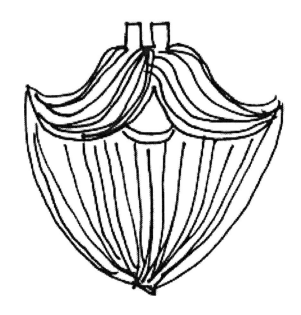

FUNNY FEET

one pair of feet   glue
tag board or construction paper   tape
scissors   markers

Funny feet can be created by tracing the outline of your child's feet on the tag board or construction paper. Cut the outline of the foot slightly larger than it really is. To make the top of the slipper cut a double of the foot but just use the toe section. Be sure to cut this section wide enough to accommodate the child's foot. This will also ensure that the slipper will stay on the child's foot. Glue the top and bottom edges together. These slippers can be colored with crayons or markers and glitter can be added. The edges can be reinforced with masking tape or colored tape.

MITTENS

one pair of hands
construction paper   markers
hole punch   glue or tape
yarn   glitter

Mittens are created very much like the funny feet project. The only difference with the mittens is that the edges are punched out all the way around (except the bottom) with a hole punch. It is important when cutting out the mittens using the shape of the hands that about an inch is added. After the holes are punched yarn is then laced through the holes in an overhand sewing type motion. After the mittens are laced together it is time to decorate with markers, glitter and glue. (This is a great project that combines creativity with a hand/eye coordination activity.)

VISORS

paper plate   markers
hole punch   scissors
yarn or string

Visors are a fun summer hat that can be created as a project for birthday parties or picnics. Mom or dad can cut the shape of the visor for the younger child. The visor pattern in the back of the book can be used to trace the shape of the visor. A hole is made at each narrow end of the visor and a sting is then tied in place to each opening. The visor is then ready to be decorated with markers, stamps and stickers.

PAPER PLATE MASK

paper plates	yarn
scissors	feathers
string	hole punch
construction paper	

To create a mask the eye, nose and mouth opening need to be cut out. This is an area where mom and dad need to do the cutting but the child certainly can help determine the shapes to be cut out. It is helpful to have a theme in mind when creating mask such as animals, monsters and people. A hole is then punched on each side above the ears and a string is tied into each hole. This is what will hold the mask on. Feather, glitter, markers or yarn can be used to decorate the mask.

TAG BOARD MASKS

tag board	scissors
markers	popsicle stick or tongue depressor
raffia or yarn	masking tape
tempera paints	

Tag board masks can be created by first cutting out the tag board into the desired shape. The eye holes, mouth and nose are then cut out. The board is then painted and decorated as desired. A handle is then tapped into place.

PAPER PLATE BONNETS

paper plate   ribbon
streamers   stapler
feathers   glue

Paper plate bonnets are fun to create in the Spring time. The bottom of the plate serves as the top of the bonnet. The top of the bonnet is decorated with feathers, streamers, glitter, buttons or any other craft materials that are available. The ribbons are then stapled on and serve as the ties that hold the bonnet on.

PIRATE HATS

black construction paper
scissors
stapler

To create a pirate hat use the pattern for the pirate hat found in the back of the book. Cut three of the pirate pieces out from the pattern. Decorate one side of each of the black papers. Decoration ideas include stickers, glitter or a feather. The corners are then staples together to form a triangle type hat. Be sure to measure before you do the final staple. These hats are great for pirate-type get togethers.

GOOGLIE GLASSES

tag board   markers
scissors   glue
colored cellophane

Googlie glasses are created by cutting out tag board in the shape of glasses. This will be a project for mom or dad or an older sibling. The Googlie Glasses pattern is located in the back of the book in the pattern section. After the glasses are cut out they need to be decorated. Small pieces of cellophane are cut out and then glued around the inside edge of the glasses. Make a hole with a hole puncher on each side of glasses. Secure a rubber band in loop fashion in each hole. These will serve as ear fasteners. Presto a great pair of shades.

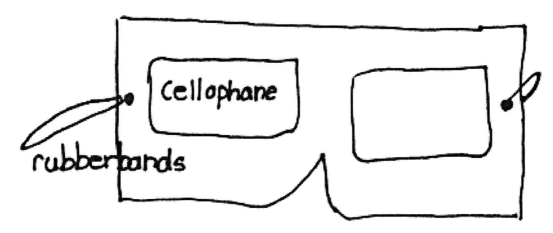

PIPE CLEANER GLASSES

three pipe cleaners any color
scissors

Pipe cleaner glasses are fun and easy to make. The pipe cleaners are twisted into two circles that are attached and then two arms are bent into shape and then attached to the eye pieces. The possibilities are limitless.

PAPER BAG VESTS

grocery bag
scissors
magic markers

The paper bag is cut up the center and a neck opening is cut at the top. Arm holes need to be cut into each side. Decorate the vest as desired.

PAPER FANS

paper any style will do
stapler

To accessorize your hats and vest be sure to cool off with a fan. The fan is created by accordion folding a piece of paper any size. When your done folding staple the handle. This is a great activity to help build hand/eye coordination.

NEWSPAPER HAT

newspaper
masking tape
markers

Paper hats are a favorite, fun and easy hat to make. To make a pirate hat use one section of a newspaper and follow the step-by-step section below.

*Take a newspaper folded in half and fold down the corners from the folded edge of the newspaper forming a point. About four inches of paper should be left uncovered at the bottom of the paper.

*Fold the two bottom edges of the newspaper towards the folded corners. Be sure to fold the bottom edge one on each side. This creates the bottom edge of the hat.

*Decorate the hat to suit your personality. Color it with markers adding your name or whatever suits your fancy. A feather can be rather dashing.

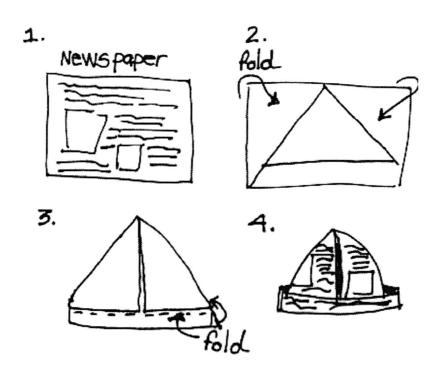

1. Newspaper

2. fold

3. fold

4.

CONE HAT

newspaper	markers
tape	glitter
streamers	glue

Cone hats are created by rolling a folded sheet of newspaper into a cone and securing it into place with tape. If desired the hat can be decorated with glue, glitter and markers and several streamers can be taped to the top of the hat. A lovely addition to the newspaper skirt.

PAPER BAG HAT

paper bag	glue
scissors	buttons
markers	fabric
feathers	yarn

To create a paper bag hat cut several inches off the top of a paper bag. The top of the bag is then rolled down. This creates a hat with a brim. Have your child decorate their hats with markers, glue, glitter, feathers, buttons, streamers, fabric or pieces of yarn. Star garland adds a festive touch to these paper bag hats as well.

NEWSPAPER TWIRLING SKIRT

newspaper	
yarn	tape

The fun part about this project is tearing the newspaper into strips. After the strips are torn they are then taped onto a piece of yarn large enough to go around the child's waist and then be tied. When complete, tie the skirt around the child's waist. This skirt is fun to wear when listening and dancing to music.

NEWSPAPER PONCHO

newspaper	scissors

To create a newspaper poncho cut a hole in the center of a large sheet of newspaper and slip the paper over the child's head. The newsprint can be decorated with crayons or markers.

Chapter 10
A Plethora of Paper Plate Projects

We have found a multitude of creative uses for paper plates at our house. As long as we have paper plates and a bottle of glue there never is a reason for boredom.

COLLAGES

Paper plates make a wonderful base for a collage. As with most collages, the potential is limitless. Reading a favorite story or listening to some favorite music can be a great inspiration when creating collage projects. Here are a few paper plate collages that we have come up with.

MAGAZINE PAPER PLATE COLLAGE

paper plate	magazines
glue	scissors

Have the child cut selected pictures from magazines. We have found it to be more interesting if a specific theme is in mind when creating the collages. We have tried animals, happy faces, favorite foods, families and favorite toys.

CONSTRUCTION PAPER PLATE COLLAGES

construction paper   paper plate
scissors
glue or paste

Shapes can be cut out of construction paper and then glued or pasted into place. Circles, squares, triangles and squares lend themselves nicely to this activity.

PAPER PLATE PIZZA

paper plate   glue
scissors   construction paper

Paper plate pizzas are created by gluing construction paper pieces on a paper plate to make it look like a pizza. Glue on a red circle for the sauce (don't forget to let the crust show) and then glue on your favorite toppings.

TEXTURED PAPER PLATE COLLAGE

paper plate
various textures such as: glue
fabric   scissors
sandpaper   wax paper
aluminum foil   gift wrap
cardboard

Various textures are glued onto the paper plate. When completed punch two holes in the top and hang by a ribbon, piece of string or rope.

CLOUD PAPER PLATE COLLAGE

paper plate   paint brush
white glue   cotton balls
blue tempera paint

We usually do this collage after we have looked at the sky and read one of our favorite picture books by David G. Shaw titled IT LOOKED LIKE SPILT MILK. To make a cloud collage you will need to mix about 1/4 cup of white glue in a disposable container. Mix the blue tempera paint with the white glue until your favorite color of sky blue is achieved. This glue/paint mixture is then used to paint the blue sky background on the paper plate. The child then places his/her cotton ball clouds in place. When the mixture is dry, the clouds will remain in place. The cotton balls can be pulled apart and glued on to represent the different types of clouds. This is truly a cloudy day activity.

WEATHER DIALS

paper plate   scissors
paper fastener   ruler
markers   piece of light weight cardboard

Weather Dials are a fun way to help the young child become aware of the weather outside. To help your child create a weather wheel divide the paper plate into four sections by drawing lines with a ruler and marker. The sections are then labeled with the words: cloudy, rainy, snow and sunshine. These words can be cut from magazines, written on by a parent or even printed on the computer and then glued on by the child. Each section is then decorated to go along with the corresponding weather. These pictures can be drawn by the child, stickers can be used or magazine pictures can be glued into place. A weather dial is created by making a 4 inch rectangle out of lightweight cardboard. One of the ends is cut into a point. Fasten the dial with a paper fastener in the center of the plate. We add a happy face to the point end to help the children remember what end is used to find the weather.

paper fastener

117

PAPER PLATE TREASURE POCKET

paper plate   stickers
hole punch   markers
yarn

Treasure pockets are created by folding a paper plate in half. Holes are then punched halfway up the sides of the plate being sure to leave the top open. Tie a piece of yarn onto each of the bottom holes. Have the child lace the yarn around the plate to make the pockets. (Putting a piece of tape onto the end of the yarn helps to make the lacing much easier.) Write the child's name on the pocket and then have them decorate their pockets with stickers.

LETTER POCKETS

two paper plates   ribbon or yarn
hole punch   markers

Letter pockets are another fun activity for the young child. Use two paper plates cutting one of them in half. Place the plates together insides facing each other. Punch holes around the edge of the plates (be sure that the holes on both plates match up). Lace the two plates together with a ribbon or string starting at the top of the plate. Be sure to leave two or three inch ends. When the plate is laced up, tie the two ends together and this will serve as the hanger for the plate.

PAPER PLATE VISORS

paper plate   hole punch
string or elastic   stickers
glitter   sequins
markers

To make this visor you will need one parent to cut out the shape of the visor from the paper plate (a pattern of the visor can be found in the pattern section of this book). A hole is then punched at each narrow end of the paper plate. Tie a piece of yarn or elastic to each of the holes. Have the child decorate the visor with the markers, glitter, sequins and glitter. We used this activity at one of my son's birthday parties. The children made their own party hats and since it was a sunny day it kept the sun out of their eyes.

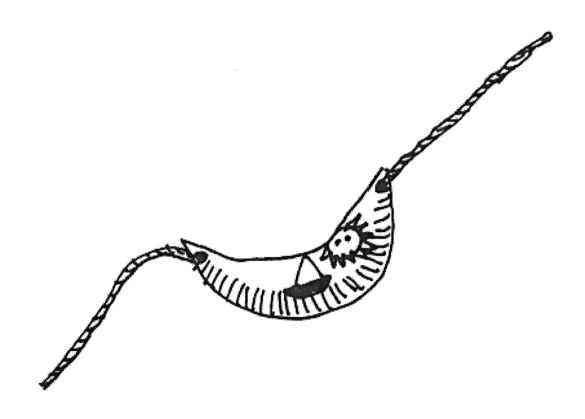

THE PAPER PLATE SPIRAL

paper plate   stapler
markers   hole punch
scissors   streamers

This activity is a fun one for the child since the spiral can be hung up from the ceiling over their bed, and it can be watched as it moves. Fortunately, this project only requires a small amount of parental intervention. A spiral needs to be drawn on the paper plate with a magic marker. The child needs to decorate the bottom of the paper plate with magic markers. The paper plate is then CAREFULLY cut along the marker lines. This is excellent cutting practice with scissors for the young child. A hole is punched into the center of the spiral and a piece of yarn is tied into place. The other end of the spiral is decorated with colored streamers.

MASKS

paper plates   markers
glue   scissors
glitter   feathers
popsicle stick or tongue depressor

Paper plates make wonderful masks too. Eyes, nose and mouth holes will need to be cut out from the paper plate. A little help from mom or date will be needed for this part of the project. The plates can then be decorated into anything the child desires. Here are a few suggestions that we have tried with great success. Paper plates lend themselves to becoming a terrific Mr. or Mrs. Sun. Glue bright colored sunshine rays around the perimeter of the plate and add glitter for interest. Glue or tape a handle in place. The paper plates also make wonderful flowers as well. Glue petals around the outside edge of the plate. Color the inside with markers or add glitter for interest. Ties can be added in place of the popsicle stick or tongue depressor handle if desired.

PAPER PLATE FRAMES

paper plate
ruler
pencil
scissors
paint brush

paint (two different colors)
sponges cut into various shapes
masking tape
ribbon

Parents need to help cut out the opening in the center of the paper plate using the pencil and ruler to get the lines even. Have the child paint the paper plate their favorite color. When the paint is dry have the child dab the moistened sponge into the other color paint. Stamp the shapes around the frame. When dry, tie a ribbon at the top for hanging and masking tape a favorite photo onto the back.

PAPER PLATE DREAM CATCHERS

paper plate
scissors
yarn

beads
hole punch
feathers

To create a dream catcher the center of the plate is removed leaving the rim. Eight holes are then punched into the rim of the paper plate about every two inches or so. The yarn in then tied to one of the holes and threaded through the hole directly across from it. Keep threading the yarn through the holes to form a star-type pattern. Beads can be added along the way. Remember simplicity is a better approach for this project. Tie a piece of yarn about 4 inches long from the bottom of the catcher and add a bead and a feather. The feather can be held in place by inserting it into the end of the bead.

PAPER PLATE TAMBOURINES

two thick paper plates	bells	streamers
hole punch	stickers	
yarn	markers	

Thicker paper plates work best for this project. This activity will require help from mom or dad. Two of the thick paper plates will need to have six holes punched out at the same location on both paper plates. The bottoms of the plates are first decorated and then six pieces of yarn that have been threaded with the bells are used to tie the paper plates together. These tambourines can be decorated for various holiday themes and are fun to make at birthday parties or if you have a parade in mind.

PAPER PLATE PUPPETS

paper plate	scissors
construction paper	
glue	

Paper plate puppets are constructed from a paper plate that has been folded in half. A narrow strip of construction paper that serves as a handle is then cut and glued on the ends near the fold of the plate. This helps the child to hold onto the plate as he brings his/her puppet to life. Features are cut and glued on to the puppet. Eyes, mouth, eyelashes, and hair are glued on the top of the plate. The inside is where the tongue and teeth are glued.

With a little imagination and a package of paper plates a plethora of projects are possible. The following are a few constructions that we have come up with at our house in our quest to fill the Paper Plate Zoo.

FISH

paper plate	scissors
tempera paint	glue
paint brush	glitter
markers	

The first step of the fish construction is to have the child paint the bottom of the paper plate. Be sure to protect any surfaces with newspaper and the child's clothing with paint smocks. Glitter can be added to the paint before it is dry. When the paint is dry, a pie piece is cut from the paper plate. This pie piece will be glued on the back of the fish as the tail. The opening which remains will serve as the fish's mouth. Draw a dot above the fish's mouth to serve as the eye. Fins can be drawn on to the fish's body.

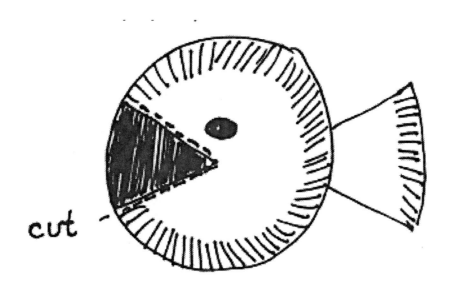

cut

JELLYFISH

paper plate glue or staple
markers or crayons streamers

A jellyfish is another type of creature that can be created with the aid of the paper plate. Color the plate with a variety of pleasant colors. We use pastels since real jellyfish have translucent bodies. Water color paints work great on this project. Cut the paper plate in half. The bottom of the paper plate is the place where the streamers are stapled or glued on. The streamers serve as the tentacles of the jellyfish. Hang the fish by tying a string through a hole at the top of the jellyfish

PAPER PLATE RABBIT

paper plate glue
two construction paper bunny ears crayons or markers
whiskers paper or pipe cleaners
nose (small pink pom-poms work great)

One plate will create a bunny head but a body can be created as well by using two paper plates of varying sizes. To make the bunny face glue the ears in place and add bunny whiskers and nose. Draw in the remaining features with the markers and crayons. If creating a body add paws to body and then glue the head to the body. Don't forget that Cotton Tail!

PAPER PLATE MICE

paper plate   glue
mouse ears   markers
tempera paint

Paper plate mice are as easy to construct as the rabbit. The only difference between the rabbit and the mouse is in the shape of the ears. Small paper plates can be used for ears. Paint can be used to color the mouse's body gray. If the entire mouse is made, a piece of yarn can be used for the animals tail.

PAPER PLATE CAT

paper plate   markers or tempera
glue   scissors

The paper plate cat can take on a variety of personalities. Painting the entire cat a solid color and then giving the cat stripes can be great fun. To complete the features of the cat give him triangle shaped ears, construction paper whiskers, eyes, nose and a mouth from markers or pieces of construction paper.

ELEPHANTS

gray paint
paper plates
gray construction paper or another plate

Elephants are also a fun paper plate creation. The first step is to paint two paper plates gray. When the paper plates are dry one of the plates is then cut into two ears and a trunk. The ears and trunk are then glued into place. The remaining features are then glued in place. Wiggly eyes can be a fun addition to this animal creation.

PANDA BEARS

two paper plates of various sizes   glue
black and white construction paper   black markers

For the head of the panda bear glue two round black ears in place on the paper plate. To make the eyes of the panda glue black circles on to the plate. Add smaller white construction paper circles in place. Add a black nose and mouth. Glue the head to the body and add four black construction paper legs with paws.

OWLS

paper plate
brown crayons
markers

Owls are made by folding a paper plate into thirds. Fold 1/3 of the paper plate half way over on the left side and then do the same on the right side. Have the child color the folded portion of the plate brown. Draw a beak and eyes at the top of the middle section on the white part. Draw talons at the bottom.

PAPER PLATE OWL FACE

paper plate
yellow construction paper
brown tempera

glue sticks
two paper baking cups

Have the child paint the back of the paper plate brown. When the paint is dry let the child glue the yellow triangle at the top middle section of the paper plate point side down. Then the paper baking cups are glued one on each side of the triangle. Small black construction paper circles, rectangles or triangles are then glued onto the cups for the eyes. Give the child a chance to try the different black shapes for the eyes to see which "look" they prefer.

Paper Plates work well for a multitude of Holiday projects as well. To find more detailed information on creating a Santa, turkey or a wreath look in chapter 8.

Ideas that worked for me.

Please send us ideas that work for you.

Humanics Learning   PO Box 7400 Atlanta, GA 30357   •   www.humanicslearning.com

Chapter 11
Nature Art

Celebrating Nature through art with the young child can be a delightful and enlightening experience. The art activities in this chapter are designed to celebrate nature. Some of the projects are constructed with nature materials while others are made to depict items found in nature. Nature walks are a terrific beginning for the activities that follow. One of our rules on our hikes is never to hurt trees and bushes. We only pick up the leaves and treasures that we find on the ground and never take anything from private property.

NATURE RUBBINGS

paper

crayons without wrappers

nature objects

tree bark

leaves

Nature rubbings can be created with a piece of lightweight paper, a crayon without its wrapper and a nature object. Tree bark is a fun nature rubbing. Just place a piece of paper on a tree trunk and then rub with a crayon. Try a variety of trees to see the differences in the bark. Autumn is a great time to do nature rubbings with the leaves. Maple and oak leaves are a favorite at our house. Vain side up will produce the most vibrant rubbing.

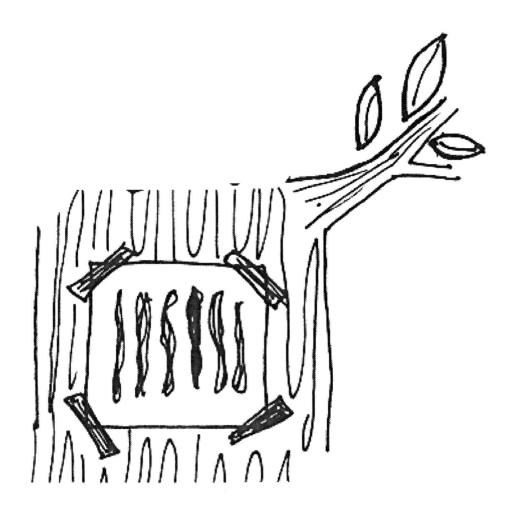

NATURE COLLAGE

glue
firm base such as a meat tray
nature objects

Nature collages begin with a nature walk with your young child. Don't forget to give your little person a Goodie Bag before you start your hike so that they can collect as many nature objects as they desire for their collage. Have your child glue their pinecones, pebbles, small twigs, leaves or whatever else they have found onto their meat trays.

131

LEAF ANIMALS

leaves of different sizes and shapes
glue
construction paper

The first step in creating Leaf Animals is to go on a leaf hunt around your neighborhood with your child. Be sure to look for leaves of different sizes, shapes, contrast and textures. (Tiny leaves work great for eyes, noses, beaks and feet.) The leaves need to be dry and flat. Some suggestions for leaf animals are owls, butterflies, frogs, foxes and turkeys.

GARDEN COLLAGES

garden magazines   scissors
glue   imagination
construction paper

Garden theme collages are fun for children to do. Try having your child create a Claude Monet Garden collage. Don't forget the Japanese bridge or the lily pads.

Reading Linnea in Monet's Garden was great fun and an inspiration for my children. Theme gardens based around roses or seasons can also be fun. As with any collage, have the child cut out pictures and then glue them in place. A picture of your child can also be glued onto the collage to put your child into the garden.

WOOD SCRAP COLLAGE

wood scraps
tongue depressors
popsicle sticks
generous amount of glue (wood glue works great)

Wood Scrap Collages are made from a variety of wood scraps. These scraps can usually be collected from any place that does any type of wood working. Be sure that the wood scraps are free of nails and rough edges that could cause slivers. Fragrant woods such as cedar and pine are fun to use. Have the child use a larger piece of wood for the base and glue a variety of small wood scraps onto the base. Popsicle sticks and tongue depressors are useful for construction as well as for spreading glue. For this project we usually give generous amounts of glue in small containers.

CLOUD COLLAGE

light blue paper
cotton balls
white tempera paint mixed with a small amount of glue

Cloud Collages are constructed from light blue paper, cotton balls, and white paint mixed with a small amount of glue. Have the child paint the light blue paper with the white-paint mixture and add the white cotton bails.

PEBBLE MOSAICS

pebbles
small piece of plywood
tacky glue or white glue

Pebble mosaics are created by having the child glue small pebbles onto a small piece of plywood. The more pebbles glued onto the plywood the better this project will look. By collecting pebbles of various colors the child will be able to create a pleasing design if they desire. Remember to let the project dry completely before it is picked up or else the pebbles will fall off. This is a project where the more glue the better.

STAINGLASS NATURE WINDOWS

variety of leaves	iron
wax paper	crayons
masking tape	grater

Nature windows are a fun project for autumn when the leaves have begun to change color. Cut two pieces of waxpaper about the same size. Place one of the sheets of waxpaper on a newspaper (about 1 inch thick). Have the child place the leaves on the waxpaper. (Mom or dad need to grate some of the crayons for the next part of this project.) Have the child add some of the grated crayon to the waxpaper with the leaves. Place the second piece of waxpaper on top. Mom or dad will need to iron the two pieces of waxpaper. The window is ready when the crayons have melted. Tape the edges of the window with masking tape and hang in the window.

SEED MOSAICS

variety of seeds	pencil or marker
white glue	firm base

Seed mosaics are fun for children to create. The designs will become more sophisticated as the child matures. Have the child draw a design on the base and then with a glue bottle outline and fill in the design. The seeds are then placed on the glue. Egg cartons work well as a way to separate the different types and colors of seeds.

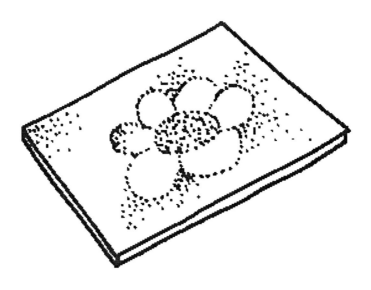

PINE CONE TURKEY

pine cones (try to find ones that are able to stand up on their ends)
feathers
pipe cleaners - use a thick brown one
glue

A treasure hunt to find pine cones is a great beginning for this project. After locating pine cones wrap the pipe cleaner around the smaller end shaping it to look like a turkey's head. Add feathers (dip the end in white glue or tacky glue) and slip in between the crevasses at the end of the cone. (Pine cones can be painted with acrylic paint and then glitter can be sprinkled on the pine cone before the turkey's head and feathers are added.)

FISH PRINTS

paint	paper
paint brush	newspaper
fish	paint smock
soapy water	

Fish Prints are a reverse printing process since the paint covered fish serves as both the printing object and the paint pad. Lay the fish on a piece of newsprint for easy clean up. Have the child paint on one side of the fish. The prints usually turn out better if an abundance of paint is not used.   Place a light-weight piece of paper on the fish and have the child gently rub the entire piece of paper. These prints look very nice mounted on colored pieces of construction paper.

LEAF PRINTING

paper towel   variety of leaves
shallow container   paper

A paint pad is created by folding several sheets of absorbent paper towels and placing this into a shallow container. Cover the paper towel with an adequate amount of tempera paint. Leaves can be used as printing devices. To make it easier to hold the leaves have the child use a pair of tweezers or a clothes pin. Try nuts, twigs and fern leaves.

TURNIP LANTERNS

turnips   nail
string   votive candle
melon ball scooper   knives

To create a turnip lantern you scoop out the inside of a turnip with a melon scooper. This will require some patience and maybe even a little help from mom and dad. Mom or dad can scoop around the edge with the pumpkin knife to get this project rolling. When the turnip is cleaned out carve a little face. Using a nail poke three holes into the top of the turnip. This will serve as a place to hang three strings from. When complete place a votive in the turnip and then hang. If hanging this outside super-vision is a necessity. (Arlene Lorella, Bellevue WA.)

BRANCH MOBILES

tree branches   objects to hang
string   scissors

Branch mobiles are made with the use of a tree branch. A nature walk can be the inspiration need-ed for this project. Several pieces of string of varying length are tied to the branch. The child can choose any item that they desire to hang from the strings such as leaves, pine cones, small rocks or twigs. For added interest two branches can be tied together to form an X. String is then tied onto the branches and objects are tied onto the ends of the strings.

EGG CARTON INSECTS

egg carton   paint brush
tempera paint   pipe cleaners
tape

The inside of the egg carton (the part that holds the eggs) make terrific spiders and caterpillars. To make these creatures separate the top from the bottom of the carton. (Paper cartons work the best.) Turn the bottom of the carton over and cut the cups into either groups of four or a single cup unit. The four cup unit will be the caterpillar's body and the single cup will be the spider. The cups are then painted your favorite insect colors. The bottom of the cups will be the top of the insect. Insert pipe cleaner legs for the spider and antenna for the caterpillar. A multitude of small pipe cleaner legs can be inserted into the body of the caterpillar if desired. Tape on the inside to hold the legs in place.

NATURE FRAMES

twigs   disposable paint brush
glue   cereal box
raffia   scissors

We have created some terrific holiday gifts with this craft idea. Cut the cereal box into a 5x7 inch frame. Use the paint brush to paint the glue onto the cardboard frame and then add twigs to cover the entire frame. Raffia makes a terrific natural hanger. Glue or tape on the raffia on the back to serve as a hanger or add magnets so that the frame can be hung on the refrigerator. Add a favorite photo by taping it in place with masking tape. Other nature objects can be used in place of the twigs and a low temperature glue gun can be substituted for the white glue if supervision is adequate.

BREAD BIRD FEEDERS

sourdough or white bread   string or ribbon
cookie cutter   nail
bird seed   knife
peanut butter

My daughter Rachael loves watching the birds eat the seeds from the bird feeders that she has made. First have your child cut out a favorite shape from a piece of bread with a cookie cutter. Make a hole near the top of the shape and insert a ribbon or string. Coat one side of the shape with peanut butter and then dip in the bird seed. Repeat the peanut butter and seed coating on the second side. Hang the feeder in a safe place for the birds to feed but a visible location so your child can enjoy their handy work.

PINE CONE BIRD FEEDER

pine cone   bird seed
peanut butter   string or ribbon

Tie a ribbon around the pine cone to serve as a hanger. Have your child cover the pine cone with peanut butter and then dip the cone in bird seed. Let your child hang their feeder in a tree or bush nearby so that they can enjoy Bird Watching. (Small pieces of Styrofoam also work well as bird feeders. Use a pipe cleaner as a hanger. Have the child coat the Styrofoam with peanut butter and then have them coat it with the bird seed.)

PAPER CUP FEEDER

paper cups   string
wooden coffee stick   lard
bird seed   plastic knife
masking tape   nail

We discovered this wonderful bird feeder on a family vacation one year while we were in Southern California. Using a nail place a small hole at the bottom of the cup. Insert a piece of sting in this hole and tape a piece of string to the inside of the paper cup to secure the string in place. Place a hole about an inch from the top of the cup and another hole parallel to this hole. Insert the coffee stirrer into the opening. This is the perch. Using the knife, cover the entire cup with lard and then cover it well with bird seed. Using rubber cloves and pressing the seed on with the hands helps to ensure that the feeder is completely covered with seed.

BIRD SEED PLAY

shallow container (dishpan size)   empty containers
large bag of bird seed   measuring cups

Playing with bird seed can be a satisfying activity for young children. Pour a large bag of bird seed into a shallow container and be sure to include a variety of measuring cups, spoons, and containers. Children will enjoying filling and dumping the containers of bird seed. This can be a messy activity so either do this outside or be sure to put a tarp on the floor where this activity will take place.

PIN WHEELS

tag board
straw
pin or tack

Pin wheels are a fun way to learn about the wind and air. Cut a six inch square out of tag board. Have your child decorate the tag board pin wheel as desired. Four five-inch cuts are made from corners to center of the square (leave center uncut). With mom or dad's help, fold the points down on the right of each cut, one at a time and overlap them in the center of the square until they are all folded. Insert a pin or tack in the middle to secure the tag board to the top of the straw.

COFFEE FILTER FLOWERS

coffee filters (Mr. Coffee style)   glue
food coloring   round piece of construction paper
wooden skewer   scissors

Coffee filter flowers are fun but food coloring stains so supervision is an absolute must with this project. Flatten the filter and then slowly add drops of food coloring. (It is fun to watch the way the colors run.) When all of the desired colors have been added, let the filter dry. Cut two circles out of construction paper. These will serve as the centers of the flowers. Place the stick (this will be the stem) onto the filter in the center. Glue the circles onto the middle of the filter (on top of the stick and filter). Glue the other circle onto the back of the filter. Green leaves can be cut out and glued or taped onto the wooden skewer.

PAPER TULIPS

paper cupcake holder (white and yellow)
glue
popsicle stick

Flatten the white cupcake paper out and then glue the yellow cup onto the center of the flattened white cup. Glue these two cups onto a popsicle stick! The yellow cup will be the center of the daffodil and the white will be the petal portion of the flower! It is fun to create several of these flowers and then insert them in a plastic flower pot that has floral foam in it. This would be a delightful gift to give to a Grandparent or perhaps someone who may need some cheering up.

PUSHING UP DAISIES

construction paper, green and two of your child's favorite colors
white glue or a glue stick
scissors
favorite picture of your child
tape measure
tape

This is a fun way to measure your child's height. First you will need to measure your child with a tape measure. Find a wall or door in your house that won't be ruined by a little tape and then mark your child's height with a pencil or piece of tape. Precut a round 6" circle for the center of the flower. (A plate works really great for this.) Precut petals out of the remaining color. For variety the petal colors can be several colors. The stem is then cut out of narrow pieces of green construction paper. Have the child glue the petals onto the flower center and then have them glue their favorite picture onto the center of the flower. (If desired, a happy face can be drawn instead of gluing on the child's picture.) Have the child glue on the stems to the flower. The flower and stems need to be the same height as the child. Write on the stem your child's name. We have written messages such as "Watching Heather Grow!" Tape the finished flower to the wall.

POMANDER

    orange, lemon or apple
    whole cloves
    ribbon

Pomanders are a fun project for children to make. We have made them for a festive and aromatic holiday gifts. Have your child choose an orange, lemon or orange. Have the child add whole cloves to the fruit until they have either filled the whole fruit or else have used the desired amount. We sometimes add ribbons to our pomanders. Add a hanger at the top by inserting several cloves into the ribbon to secure it into place.

SACHETS

    small piece fabric or netting
    ribbon
    potpourri (homemade or store bought)

The piece of fabric or netting is cut into a circle about 6 inches in diameter. Place a handful of the potpourri mixture onto the fabric. Help the child gather the fabric into a bundle and then tie a bow into place. A small flower can be added for a special touch. Have your child place their sachet in their dresser drawer or give it as a gift.

POTPOURRI

    nature walk   mini pine cones
    scented rose petals   pine needles
    cinnamon sticks

One year we decided to make potpourri for a holiday gift. A nature hunt through our neighborhood was a great way to get started. Our rule is that only materials found on the ground could be used. Collecting scented rose petals in a wicker basket is a great way to let the air circulate and dry out the petals. Add small pine cones, eucalyptus leaves, scented geranium leaves, small pieces of bark. Color, texture and scent combine to make a pleasant potpourri. The materials should not be mixed together if they are wet. It is best to let the flower petals dry out first. Apples and oranges can be sliced thinly and then air dried to be placed into a mixture of potpourri. This will be a process that may take several days but would be interesting for children to watch. Cinnamon works well with the fruit mixtures. (Special fragrant oils can be purchased at craft stores and then be added to the potpourri.)

Ideas that worked for me.

Please send us ideas that work for you.

Humanics Learning   PO Box 7400 Atlanta, GA 30357   •   www.humanicslearning.com

Pattern Section
Patterns for Your Projects.

cut side
seams of
bag to x's

cut out

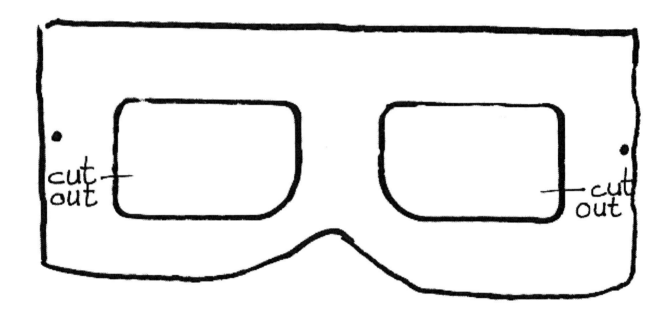

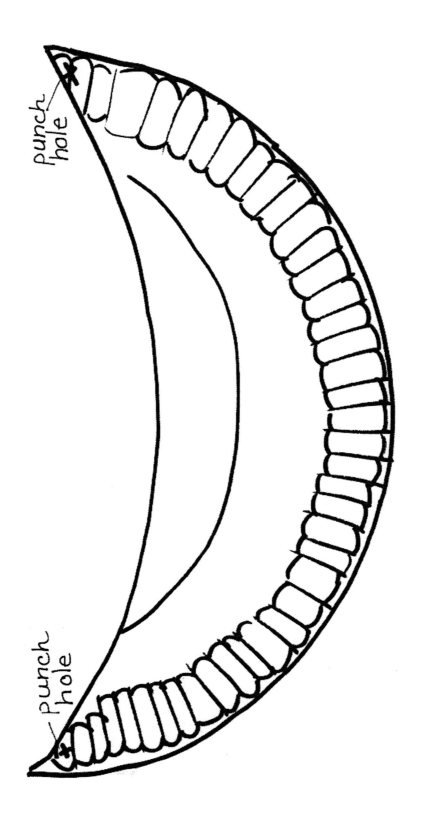

punch
hole

punch
hole

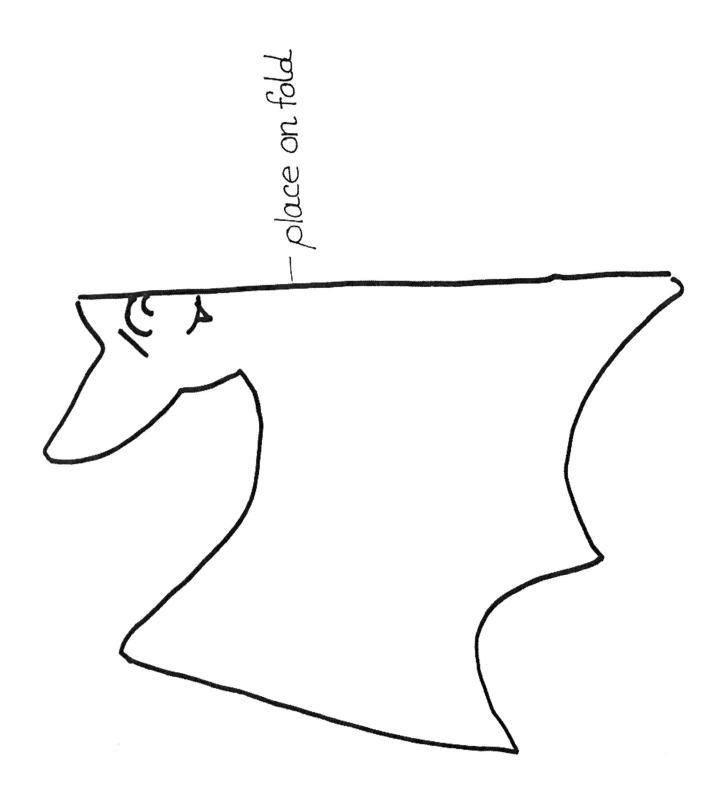

place on fold

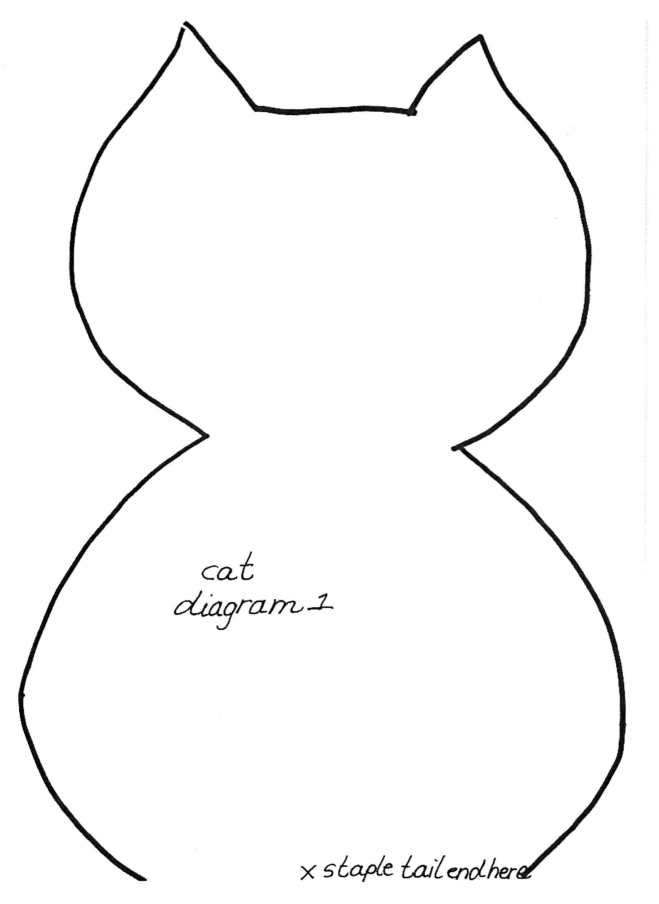

cat
diagram 1

x staple tail end here

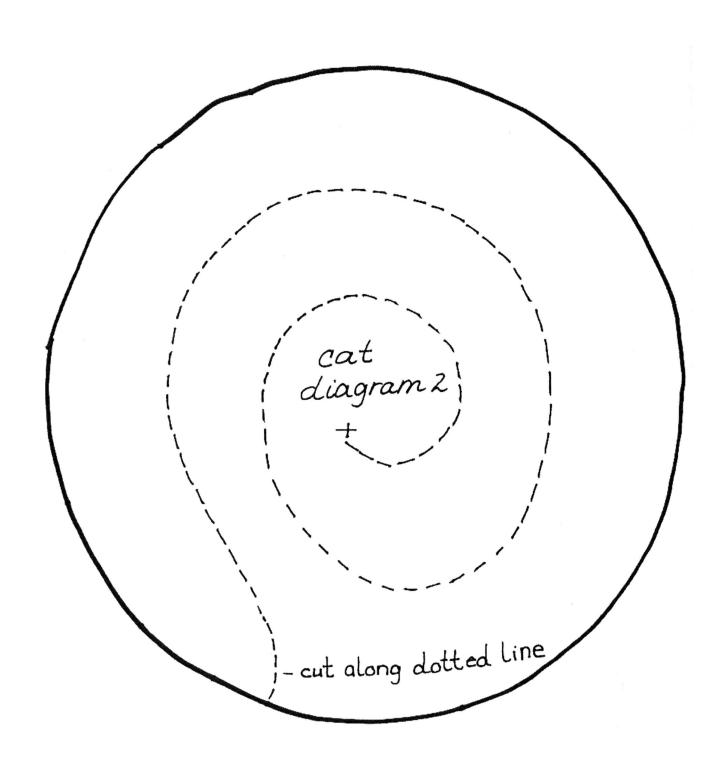

cat
diagram 2

— cut along dotted line

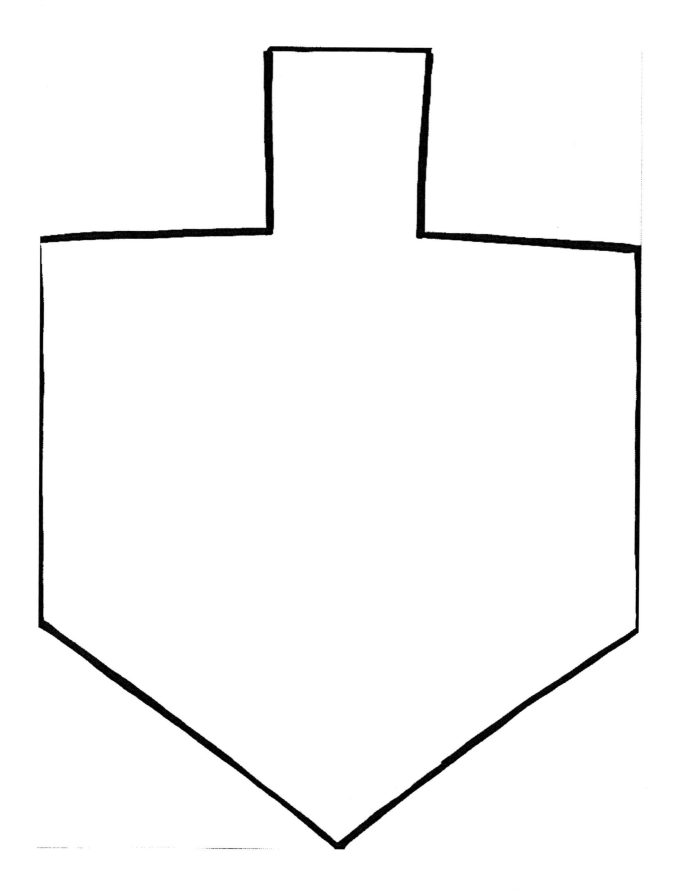

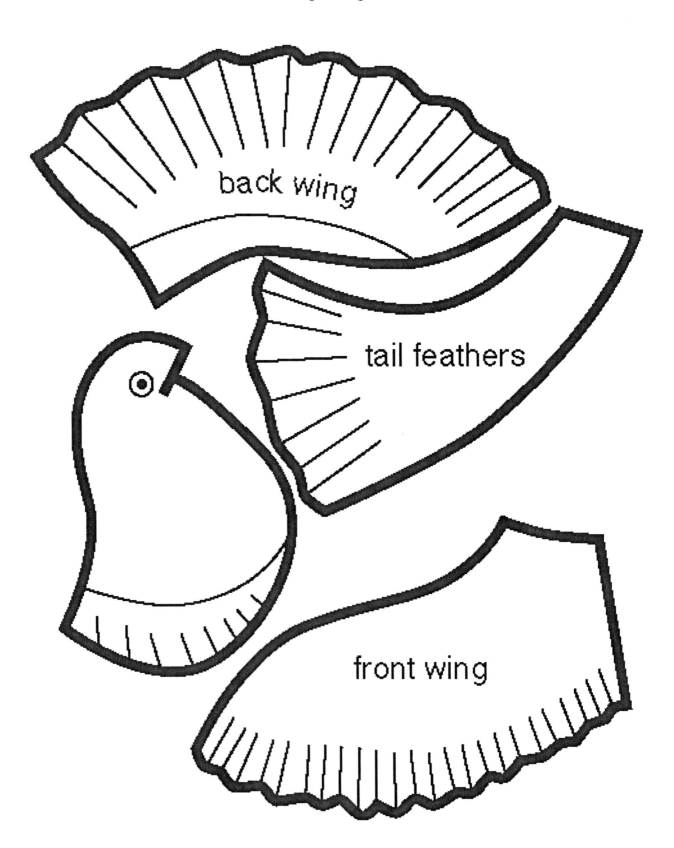

back wing

tail feathers

front wing

DATE DUE

CPSIA information can be obtained at www.ICGtesting.com
Printed in the USA
LVOW091743120213

319779LV00001B/85/A

9 780893 343002